THE
JEWISH
HOLIDAY
BAKER

THE
JEWISH
HOLIDAY
BAKER

JOAN NATHAN

Illustrated by Emma Celia Gardner

SCHOCKEN BOOKS
NEW YORK

Portions of this work were originally published in somewhat different form
in *Moment Magazine* and *The New York Times*.

Grateful acknowledgment is made to the following
for permission to reprint previously published and unpublished material:

Edda Servi Machlin: Recipes for "Italian Matzah," "Il Bollo," and "Ceciarchiata Taiglach"
are adapted from *The Classic Cuisine of the Italian Jews,* vol. 1, by Edda Servi Machlin (Giro Press,
Croton-on-Hudson, N.Y., 1981). Adapted by permission of the author.

Schocken Books Inc.: Excerpts from *The Five Books of Moses: The Schocken Bible*, vol.1,
translated by Everett Fox. Copyright © 1995 by Schocken Books Inc.
The excerpts appear on pages 4, 5, 15, 16, 55, 79, 95, 155, 156, and 175.
Reprinted by permission of Schocken Books Inc., distributed by Pantheon Books,
a division of Random House, Inc.

Library of Congress Cataloging-in-Publication Data
Nathan, Joan.
The Jewish holiday baker / Joan Nathan.
p.   cm.
Includes index.
ISBN 0-8052-4142-6
1. Baking. 2. Cookery, Jewish. 3. Jews—United States—Social
life and customs. I. Title.
TX763.N32   1997
641.8'15—dc21   97-9775
CIP

Random House Web Address: http://www.randomhouse.com

BOOK DESIGN BY FEARN CUTLER
ILLUSTRATIONS BY EMMA CELIA GARDNER

Printed in the United States of America
First Edition
2 4 6 8 9 7 5 3 1

To my mother, Pearl Nathan,
who introduced me to the joys of baking

If a man says no more than "How beautiful is this bread! Blessed be He who is everywhere for having created it," that is sufficient blessing over the bread.

A *midrash*

CONTENTS

ACKNOWLEDGMENTS

I am grateful to a number of people, most prominently Arthur Samuelson, my editor at Schocken Books, for encouraging me to write a book about Jewish baking, one of my favorite ways of transmitting traditions to my children. Mark Furstenberg, the founder of Marvelous Market in Washington, D.C., and the catalyst for great bread in the nation's capital, helped me narrow the subject by suggesting that I write about a baker's dozen of Jewish bakers the world over. And I am grateful to Susan Lescher, my agent, who as usual was there when I needed her.

Two writers have been extremely helpful to me—and to countless others— because of their books on baking (and Jewish baked delicacies): George Greenstein, author of *Secrets of a Jewish Baker* (The Crossing Press, 1993), and Maida Heatter, whose many baking books have taught a whole generation of Jews and non-Jews how to make traditional Jewish pastries. It was she who put rugelach on the culinary map. I encourage everyone to read their books.

Manfred Loeb, Washington's retired Jewish baker par excellence, whose recipes have been featured in my books *The Jewish Holiday Kitchen* and *Jewish Cooking in America,* spent hours with me in the kitchen, helping me to master the techniques of making rye breads and Danish.

I especially want to thank the bakers featured in this book: Ann Amernick, Berish Brizel, Florence and Serge Finkelsztajn, Zohar Cohen-Nehemia Halleen, Andra Tunick Karnofsky, Jeannie Lazinsky, Michael London, Edda Servi Machlin, Josiane and Alan Mansoura, Ben Moskovitz, Irwin Shlafman, Helen Silverberg, and Jack Wayne. Not only did they share recipes with me, but they also shared their stories. My hope is that this book will keep their traditions alive, as well as those of the late Alex Lichtman, Lisl Nathan Regensteiner, and Elisabeth Rosenfeld. Their children Hannah Greenwood, Cissie Klavens, Max and Dorothy Regensteiner, and Ivan, Lisette, Pablo, and Peter Span have all graciously shared anecdotes and recipes with me.

Many others helped me as well and I wish to express my gratitude to them: Jelena Blumenberg, Dalia Carmel, Frank Carollo, Paula Gerson, Ellen Gold, Carol Goldberg, Seth Greenberg, Karen Gundersheimer, Trish Hall, Jennifer Herman, Sara Kittrie, Dalya Luttwak, Congressman Sander Levin, Professor Pamela Nadell, Phyllis Richman, Trina Rubenstein, Meir Shalev, Louis Statzer, Cathy Sulzberger, Mark Talisman, Susan Toffler, Ari Weinzweig, and Rabbi Jeff and Jody Wohlberg. As with my other books, Peggy Pearlstein at the Hebraic section of the Library of Congress assisted me with my research. My assistant, Eve Lindenblatt, tirelessly helped me test and retest recipes, and Suzi Arensberg, Joan Michel, and Jennifer Turvey shepherded me through the journey of this book.

Last, but certainly not least, I owe a great debt to my family. My three children, Daniela, Merissa, and David, critiqued each batch of babka, bialys, and bagels, giving me very honest criticism, as only teenagers can! My husband, Allan, accustomed by now to the obsession that surrounds writing a cookbook, helped me with quality control, editing, and keeping on an even keel during this lengthy process.

THE
JEWISH
HOLIDAY
BAKER

INTRODUCTION

W hile testing recipes for my *Jewish Holiday Kitchen* (Schocken Books, 1979) nearly twenty years ago, I asked my late aunt Lisl to show me how she braided *berches,* the challah she had grown up with in southern Germany (see pages 56–58 for more about her and southern German cooking traditions). When she arrived at my home, I placed the dough I had prepared for her on the kitchen table. My aunt looked at it and protested that she had not braided bread for over forty years, since she had left Germany. But to her amazement, as soon as her fingers touched the soft dough, they "knew." It was as if she'd been doing it every week. Nimbly she braided three bottom strands, then three smaller top strands, in the German Friday night tradition. That is the magic of working with dough.

From my own childhood I remember how much I liked to help my mother press the buttery *mürbeteig* dough into a pie pan for the *zwetschgenkuchen,* the Italian plum tart we served for Rosh Hashanah. And I wanted to be the one to arrange the plum slices in pretty concentric circles. Now my children squabble over this task.

Baking is a great way to transmit a culture. Not only does baking fill the kitchen with wonderful aromas; it also provides that relaxed family time when, while working with your hands, you can comfortably ease into conversation, a challenge in most households today. And the results linger: homemade challah and honey cake carry an important message for everyone. It is particularly gratifying to make something out of that formless substance, flour. The Jewish people have been doing that ever since Sarah first baked those cakes for Abraham.

Here is a memory I have from Israel: An elderly woman from Morocco's Atlas Mountains wakes at 4:00 a.m. on Friday morning; she mixes water, yeast, flour, salt, and a sprinkling of anise and sesame seeds; she kneads and shapes the dough. She fires up an outdoor clay-and-straw oven with olive wood. By the time the dough has risen, the fire is ready for baking and she places flat stones on the flame. Then she pulls off a piece of dough, the challah. (Eventually, this challah came to be defined as the Sabbath loaf itself.) In Numbers 15:18–21 Moses was told that, upon entering the Land, the Israelites must set aside this challah as a tribute to the Lord. "From the premier-product of your kneading-troughs, you are to give to God a contribution throughout your generations." Later, this offering of the "first of the dough" was made to the priests at the Temple in Jerusalem, analogous to the farmer's offering of first fruits. With the destruction of the Temple, this offering of the challah was transferred to the home.

Following this ancient biblical injunction, the woman tosses the piece of dough into the fire. Then she forms round loaves, and she glazes them with egg, so they are different from everyday bread, called *lechem* in Hebrew.

I watched this ritual recently in Beit Shean, where this woman, who neither reads nor writes, now lives. Her robust, crusty loaf was very different from the Moroccan Jewish bread I had tasted at a Sabbath dinner in Marrakesh. Though also spiked with anise and sesame seeds, that bread had been sweeter, enriched with eggs, and oval in shape. Ashkenazic (Eastern European, Yiddish-speaking) Jews call their Sabbath bread challah; Moroccan women and other Sephardim (Ladino-speaking Jews of the Iberian peninsula and the Levant) call theirs *pane de Sabato* or *pain de Shabbat,* "bread of the Sabbath."

The primitive bread of the woman from the Atlas Mountains tells us much about her life and origins; it also is the story of a people. Presented in this book, the more sophisticated variety of this Moroccan bread, the Italian *bollo,* reveals another step in the wanderings of Sephardic Sabbath bread and its spices from Spain to Morocco to Italy and to the United States. Through this bread and others described here come the stories of the Jewish people, past and present. Because traditions erode more rapidly under the pressure of modern technology, it is important to preserve many of the older recipes before they vanish.

It is also valuable to consider baking from a seasonal point of view, remembering the times of the year in ancient Israel. Jews still make sweet things at Rosh Hashanah in September and October, not only to denote a sweet New Year but also to use jam made from the season's dates, grapes, and honey. At Purim we have *mishloach manot,* gifts of at least two different ready-to-eat foods, each of which requires a different blessing, and a specified amount of a liquid. Coming usually in March, Purim is a holiday replete with cookies made to use up the year's flour before Passover begins. At Shavuot in May, cheesecakes and cheese-filled Danish are traditional, as this is the time of year when cows and goats produce more milk.

The Beginnings of Jewish Breads

Consider the challah. Whether it is flat like pita or six-strand-braided and rich with eggs, or even oval like the Italian *bollo,* the prayers and customs that accompany the *mitzvah* of making a special bread for the Sabbath are the same the world over. They link the present to the time of the Book of Leviticus, when God instructed Moses to place two rows of six challot each on a table before the Lord in the tent of meeting. For more than four thousand years since, Jews have been making or buying some form of challah every Sabbath.

In Genesis, as a sign of hospitality, a bread offering is made crucial. Abraham tells Sarah: "Quick, three measures of choice flour! Knead it, make bread cakes!" (Genesis 18:6). Of course, this bread was unleavened bread, the bread of the desert. The Hebrews learned about leavening later, in Egypt. Their bread, either of barley or wheat, was thin and flat. Made from flour ground between two stones and mixed with water, it was stretched thin and then put flat on a stone slab and baked over a fire or between layers of slow-burning camel dung. It is the bread still baked in the desert at least twice a day by the Bedouin in smaller rounds, very much like the original matzah and the cakes that Sarah made for Abraham.

When the Jews settled and began baking bread, their best was of wheat, *kemach solet,* or "essence of flour," which they used as offerings with the purest olive oil in the Temple of Jerusalem and as bread for the rich. Barley was used for bread by the poor and for horse feed. To make barley bread palatable, ground lentils, beans, and millet were added. At first, Jewish wives and their daughters tended the ovens; later, maidservants helped. Still later, when Jews became city-dwellers, men tended the ovens and women baked the bread. Bakers' Street still exists in the Old City of Jerusalem, and in the days of Nehemiah, the Tower of Ovens stood in the wall surrounding the city. The Tower of Ovens was the place where bread was baked, because the smoke would blacken the buildings of the town if the fires were inside.

Baking and Religious Dietary Laws

The written code of religious dietary laws governs baking as well as general cooking. Because mixing milk and meat in the same meal is prohibited, baked goods in an observant Jewish home are labeled either dairy or parve (neutral). The kind of fat used in baked goods is very important. With dairy meals, butter, cheese, and milk can be used, but parve baked goods for meat meals present a challenge. In the ancient world, olive oil was used as a fat in baking and still is in some countries around the Mediterranean. In Central and Eastern Europe, Jews often baked with butter, coconut oil, or palm oil until recent times. Others used meat or poultry drippings, particularly rendered goose fat. In the 1906 edition of *Aunt Babette's Cook Book*, published in Chicago, Aunt Babette gave a recipe for a family pie crust in which she wrote: "Take one cup of nice drippings and mix with goose, duck or chicken fat. In the fall and winter, when poultry is plentiful and fat, you should save all drippings for pie crust. If you have neither of the above, use rendered meat fat (I do not mean suet—that is horrid!—but genuine meat fat); use half butter; if you consider this 'trefa,'* use all fat." On another page she advises clarifying butter when it is plentiful in June to use for the rest of the year. Four years after that book was published, Procter and Gamble invented Crisco, a vegetable substance that could be used in parve baking; ads claimed "the Hebrew Race had been waiting 4,000 years for it." Today, in the United States, with the availability of parve margarines, non-dairy creamers, and vegetable shortenings, we can make most baked goods parve.

The Stories Behind This Book

The Jewish Holiday Baker offers portraits of a baker's dozen of Jewish bakers and their families with more than fifty favorite recipes. Many bakers today make challah and bagels, but that doesn't make them Jewish. To me, a Jewish baker is someone who grew up with a sense of Jewish identity that is transmitted through the traditional breads and other baked goods. This is a personal book filled with stories and baking lore from people I have met and admired through the years and a few I have discovered through my travels. I have tried to include a geographical and ethnic mix of bakers, both home

---

* *Trefa,* or *treyf,* means not kosher.

cooks and professionals. The impetus for the book itself sprang from the wandering art of Jewish baking.

In 1995, when I was on assignment to interview Diana Kennedy, the authoritative writer on Mexican cuisine, in a tiny village of four hundred people, three and a half hours from Mexico City, the last person I expected to meet was a Jew, much less a Jewish baker. While staying at a pension I started talking with Lisette Span, the owner, in French because I do not speak Spanish. When I told her I wrote primarily about Jewish food, she showed me a cookbook in Spanish that her late mother-in-law, Elisabeth Rosenfeld, had written. Mrs. Rosenfeld, a Holocaust survivor from Yugoslavia, cooked and baked to support her family in Mexico City after the war; it was she who taught the elite of Mexico City, including Diana Kennedy, how to stretch strudel.

A year later I went to Boston to interview the daughter of another Jewish strudel baker. Cissie Klavens's grandparents and parents had run Mrs. Herbst's Bakery in New York from 1935 until it closed in 1986. Hungarian-born Alex Lichtman, the chief baker and Cissie Klavens's father, carefully transmitted to his wife the bakery's recipes for dobos torte, kugelhopf, *pogacsa,* and yeast-based hamantashen shortly before his death. After our meeting, Mrs. Klavens went to a wedding in New York. Seated at her table was the pension owner from Mexico, who during the course of the conversation mentioned that an American wanted her to share recipes from her late mother-in-law, Elisabeth Rosenfeld, for a book on Jewish baking. This coincidence, later related to me, created a life of its own for this book. These two family stories spanned two continents and four countries—Hungary, Yugoslavia, Mexico, and the United States.

Like Alex Lichtman and Elisabeth Rosenfeld, other Jewish bakers have used their craft as a way to support their families. Michael London, a baker in upstate New York outside Saratoga Springs, grew up in Brooklyn and apprenticed in some of New York's great Jewish bakeries, among them William Greenberg, Jr., and the now-closed Eclair Bakery. Others—like Ann Amernick, the first Jewish assistant pastry chef in the White House, Zohar Cohen-Nehemia Halleen, a home baker and twenty-sixth-generation Jerusalemite, and Andra Tunick Karnofsky, of Chicago's Heavenly Hallah—come from families where baking was part of growing up. Several of these bakers also remember the once-communal aspect of bread making. Ben Moskovitz, owner of the Star Bakery in Oak Park, Michigan, grew up in a small Czech village; his family had the oven to which the Jewish villagers brought their bread to be baked.

No book on Jewish baking would be complete without a bagel, today an icon of American culture. To me, the best come from Montreal, at the wood-fired-oven bakery called Fairmount Bagel Bakery. Most of the French Canadian customers certainly do not know that bagels were first made in Krakow and Kiev by Jewish bakers.

The art of Jewish baking is filled with ingenuity and adaptability. My favorite challah in Jerusalem comes from Brizel's Bakery on Mea Shearim Street. The recipe for this crusty, slightly sweet bread traveled from Poland to Jerusalem a hundred years ago. I have tasted similar versions in Brooklyn and Detroit and at Finkelsztajn's Bakery in the Marais district of Paris. The Finkelsztajn family, originally from Lodz, serves as well traditional Jewish Polish cheesecake made with a French white cheese and a *fluden* made with figs and spiked with a Tunisian liqueur. Over two hundred years ago, the Mansoura family started making Syrian *ka'ak* (pretzel-like rings) and *adjwah* (date-filled crescents) in Aleppo; later their base was Cairo, now it's Brooklyn.

In addition to economic and political migrations, the Holocaust, more than any other event in modern history, displaced thousands of Jewish bakers. Like Elisabeth Rosenfeld and Ben Moskovitz, Edda Servi Machlin, author of *The Classic Cuisine of the Italian Jews,* volumes 1 and 2 (Giro Press, 1981, 1992), and my aunt Lisl Nathan Regensteiner would have stayed in Europe their entire lives had it not been for Hitler. From all these people we discover not only great recipes and the legacy of baking, but also Jewish history.

About Dough and Baking

This is a book with recipes that anyone can make. Except for a few challenging ones, such as the dobos torte (pages 126–28), there should be few problems. As someone who likes to bake but has to fit it into a busy life, I have tried to simplify these recipes.

There is waiting time in baking, so try to relax and enjoy that time. You can also do as I do: let the baking fit your schedule. When I am making challah, for example, I often start the dough on Thursday afternoon or evening, let it rise in the refrigerator overnight, bring it to room temperature at a moment convenient for me, and then bake it. I also frequently braid a month of challahs at a time, freeze them before the final rising, and bake them as needed. Whenever possible I have indicated the points in a recipe where you can stop the action. Don't be daunted by a recipe like Elisabeth Rosenfeld's start-from-scratch strudel (see pages 177–78). It is great fun to stretch the dough out, and a few rips won't matter—they are easily patched up.

About covering the dough: you don't want dough to dry out while it is rising. If your kitchen is dry, cover your dough with a slightly damp towel. If it is humid, use a dry towel. You can also use a large clear plastic bag (one made for food storage purposes) to cover the entire bowl, making sure that the dough can breathe. You can also cover the dough loosely with plastic wrap.

Finally, don't be afraid of making yeast-based recipes. See how much pleasure—not to mention release of tension—you will feel in kneading dough, and what pride you will have in the final product.

Baking Ingredients

Wherever possible I have given the choice of using butter or parve margarine to make the recipe either dairy or parve and have marked the recipes with a **D** or **P**.

At the end of the book there is a shopping guide to great bakeries and mail-order sources, plus a glossary of foreign food terms.

I have used the flours the bakers suggested. Low-gluten cake flour, often mixed with all-purpose flour, yields flaky crusts; for doughs that need more gluten—a protein substance that gives dough an elastic quality for stretching and molding—high-gluten and bread flours are recommended. Don't let this variety of flours scare you away, however. Except for strudel and bagels, where high-gluten flour does make a big difference, you can always use all-purpose flour if that's what is in your kitchen. (I think *unbleached* all-purpose is the best here.) Just remember that you may need a little bit more all-purpose flour than bread flour in your recipes and more cake flour than all-purpose. As for yeast, I say 1 scant tablespoon or 1 package, which is actually 2¾ teaspoons yeast.

As you explore this book, keep in mind that if you are going to take the time to make baked goods, you should be sure that every calorie is a good one. I suggest baking with the best ingredients, such as good imported chocolate, top-quality butter, real vanilla extract, and good active dry yeast (which I buy in bulk by mail order from Walnut Acres, or from stores like the Price Club, because the yeast is much cheaper and seems to be stronger than in the individual packets). A baking *bubbemeise* (old wives' tale) is that you need to proof active dry yeast with sugar and water for 10 minutes. Don't— it is a wasted step with our modern yeasts. It used to be necessary in the old days, but not with today's expiration dates.

Equipment

You will see that all the bakers in this book make use of an electric mixer and a food processor. I do, too. The electric mixer, which can very efficiently mix the doughs called for here, and even knead them, must be a good, heavy one, and it should be equipped with a paddle (for stirring heavy batters), a whisk (for egg whites and light batters), and a dough hook (for kneading). All food-

paddle   whisk   dough hook   steel blade

processor dough work can be done with a food processor fitted with a steel blade, but when there is a particularly large amount of dough, you'll need to halve or cut in thirds the amount put in—and repeat your steps. So for large-volume recipes, I recommend the mixer or, of course, a large bowl, a wooden spoon, a pastry blender for mixing sugar into butter, and your hands for the kneading.

Many of these recipes call for a combination of machine and hand work. Should you want to do the entire process by hand, just extend the mixing and kneading time; you'll learn fast to appreciate the feel of the dough you are working. The recipes here do try as much as possible to describe that feel.

I also want to mention two hand tools that I find essential as well as beautiful: a one-piece, tapered rolling pin (the French kind), and a steel pastry scraper with a wooden handle. The rolling pin lets you really feel the dough moving underneath it, and the pastry scraper gets up all those dough scraps in a flash. Both are great fun to use.

THE SABBATH

THE ULTIMATE CHALLAH,
from Brizel's Bakery and Jack Wayne

HEAVENLY WHOLE-WHEAT CHALLAH,
from Andra Tunick Karnofsky

YEMENITE KUBBANAH,
from Zohar Cohen-Nehemia Halleen

JERUSALEM BOYOS,
from Zohar Cohen-Nehemia Halleen

NEW YORK BIALYS,
from Michael London

WILLIAM GREENBERG, JR.'S SCHNECKEN,
with help from Michael London

CHOCOLATE BABKA,
from Ben Moskovitz

KUCHEM-BUCHEM,
from Jeannie Lazinsky

KICHEL,
from Ben Moskovitz

Between me and the Children of Israel a sign it is, for the ages,
for in six days God made the heavens and the earth, but on the seventh day
he ceased and paused-for-breath.

EXODUS 31:17

O n Friday night, every observant Jewish family the world over recites three blessings before dinner. The first is over the candles, thanking God for sanctifying the Sabbath, the second is over wine in thanks for the fruit of the vine, and the third is over two covered loaves of challah. This last prayer gives thanks to God as *hamotzi lechem min ha'aretz*—"the one who brings forth bread from the earth." Then a morsel of bread for each person at the meal is broken off before the words *Shabbat shalom* (Sabbath peace) are spoken. The blessing over the bread at the beginning of every meal connects Jews continuously to the food that grows in the earth and to God. On the Sabbath, the bread becomes a symbol of holiness.

This bread and the Sabbath are central to Judaism and to the routine of weekly life. In keeping with the Fourth Commandment, no work—even cooking, no matter how much people might enjoy it—can be done on the seventh day. With no cooking allowed for twenty-four hours, all food is prepared ahead of time for three special meals: Friday evening, Saturday midday, and Saturday late afternoon, before dusk. Although today there are no set rules for these meals, Friday night and Saturday midday are traditionally meat meals and Saturday evening is a light dairy meal.

Festive breads and baked goods, separating the Sabbath from the rest of the week, are prepared ahead for these three meals and have become an integral part of Jewish life. Thus, many American Jews, whether religious or not, are accustomed to eating a sweet braided challah and perhaps a babka on the Sabbath. For many, these special dishes are a reminder of the purity of the day of rest, as well as a remembrance of the historic gastronomic deprivation of Eastern European Jews who lived on black bread during the week.

Many traditions include an "overnight" baked bread for Saturday breakfast, such as the Yemenite *kubbanah,* or flaky filled buns like the Turkish *boyos* or the sticky German schnecken. Whatever the bread, the sharing of it on the Sabbath will be enhanced immeasurably by the making of it.

The Sabbath Bread

"You are to take flour and are to bake it (into) twelve loaves, two tenth-measures shall be the one loaf" (Leviticus 24:5). God instructed Moses to place these round loaves—two rows of six *challot* each—on a table before Him in the tent of meeting: "Sabbath day (by) Sabbath day he is to arrange it before the presence of God, regularly, from the Children of Israel as a covenant for the ages" (Leviticus 24:8).

After the Romans destroyed the Temple in Jerusalem in 70 C.E., the home table became a metaphor for God's table; it was likened to the altar in the Temple. And the Sabbath bread became a sacred offering from every family.

By the eighteenth century, when twisted breads had come into vogue in Central and Eastern Europe, the twelve round loaves of bread in Leviticus became two loaves with at least six humps from the braids in each. Some bakers still carefully braid the challah dough so that six humps will show in each of the two traditional loaves used on the Sabbath. There are several explanations for the two loaves. One is that they represent the double portion of manna that the Lord provided on the sixth day in the wilderness during the forty years of wandering, so there would be enough for the Sabbath and the Israelites would not need to collect it on the day of rest (Exodus 16:22–23). Another is that the two loaves represent two different versions of the Fourth Commandment. In Exodus 20:8, the words are to "remember the Sabbath day, to hallow it." In Deuteronomy 5:15, in the repetition of the Ten Commandments, the Jews are reminded that they were slaves in Egypt, but that "God took you out from there with a strong hand and with an outstretched arm; therefore your God commands you to observe the day of Sabbath."

The Sabbath bread closest to that of the ancient Israelites is baked by Iraqi and many Sephardic Jews. It is a flat bread, more like pita, sometimes in a larger size than that of everyday bread. In many Israeli homes today, this Iraqi, Yemenite, or Kurdish flat bread sits side by side with the European sweet challah, and the breads are blessed together. The sweetened loaf, developed much later, was not just a Jewish phenomenon. The Greeks have an egg-rich braided bread at Easter; so do the Portuguese and the Russians.

Berches, possibly a corruption of the Hebrew word for "blessing" (*b'rachah*), is the savory German Jewish Sabbath loaf of two layers of three-braided strands. My father ate a potato-based *berches* as a child in Augsburg, Germany. So did Jews I've met who lived as far away as Budapest.

The changes continued . . . A round challah at Rosh Hashanah became a symbol of long life. Some people added saffron and raisins to it. Others added more symbolism. In certain Russian towns, the bread was imprinted with the shape of a ladder, symbolizing the ascent to God on high. (A *midrash,* or explanatory story, states that on Rosh Hashanah the "Holy One, blessed be He, sits and erects ladders; on them God lowers one person and elevates another.") In Ukraine, perhaps in Kulikow, a town known for breads, Rosh Hashanah challah was baked in the form of a bird, symbolizing the protection of God's people, as stated in Isaiah 31:5: "As birds hovering (over their fledglings), so will the Lord of hosts protect Jerusalem." Jews from Lithuania baked challah topped with a crown, in accordance with the words of the great liturgical poet Eleazar Kalir: "Let all crown God." And the food impresario George Lang recalls his mother's regular Friday night challah from Hungary—"elaborate . . . a bird with peppercorn eyes, grapes. It was wonderful, mellow, and had a slightly sweet dough."

Many challah traditions were lost as a result of the Holocaust and Soviet religious suppression. When I visited the Soviet Union a few years before its breakup, I kept searching for a sweet Russian challah. In Tbilisi, at the home of a *chazzan* (cantor) from one of the few remaining synagogues, I tasted a homemade round white loaf, with no sweetening. In Moscow, contrary to my expectations, I found no challah. Nor did I see any in Vilnius. But someone translated a small item for me from a Lithuanian newspaper. "Remember that challah bread," it read. "How we used to like it. Perhaps now that there is *perestroika* some bakery will bake it again for us." They did not. The Jewish bakers of Lithuania are no more.

Challah Hopping in Jerusalem

Jerusalem is the city I explored, starting one morning at five o'clock, to find the ultimate challah.

My odyssey began at an Iraqi bakery in the Bukharan quarter, one of the oldest neighborhoods outside the Old City, built and financed in the late nineteenth century by Jews from Bukhara in Central Asia. The wood-fired oven of this hole-in-the-wall bakery included a concave clay cover. The dough, stretched by hand, was placed on a gigantic pot holder and then pressed onto that clay cover, to be peeled off a few minutes later, when cooked. This crisp flat bread, popular in the holy city, is eaten by Iraqis for all meals, even the Sabbath. Although it includes leaven, it is not much different from the earliest matzah of the ancient Jews, and is most like the bread offered in the Temple in Jerusalem.

A few blocks away I visited Nahama, a Persian bakery, with a more sophisticated wood-fired oven. Here the bakers were forming the same dough as the Iraqis into more bulbous oval shapes, pressing their fingers into the tops, and then transferring the loaves to long wooden paddles, which they used to put the loaves into the oven and then remove them. Challah for Persians, I learned, like the bread of the Iraqis, is just a different form of their everyday bread. "Go around the corner for your sweet challah," advised a customer.

My next stop was in a narrow alley at Lendner's Bakery, which specializes in Romanian-style challah. Matti Lendner, a third-generation baker, showed me his white brick turn-of-the-century wood-fired oven. A baker was working in the pit created below the door of the oven.

Matti Lendner is continuing a tradition started by his grandfather, Moshe Dov Lendner, who came as an early religious pioneer to bake bread in Jerusalem at a time when most religious Jews went there to die. Moshe Lendner conveniently located his bakery next to his synagogue. Every day at 3:00 a.m., he heated the sanctuary before he mixed his dough. Then he returned to pray with other congregants while the dough was rising.

Lendner's challah incorporates yeast, sugar, water, and flour. In Jerusalem at the turn of the century, when people were poor and mostly dependent on outside contributions, eggs and sugar were out of the question. "In my family's part of Romania," said Matti as he shellacked his loaves with a mixture of cornstarch and water, "challah rarely included eggs. It was already a luxury to have a bread with white flour for the Sabbath. Most Jerusalem challot today do not include eggs."

"Baking and prayer are very compatible"

Berish Brizel

Still in search of a crusty egg challah, I walked toward Migdania Brizel (Brizel's Bakery) on ultra-Orthodox Mea Shearim Street. Black-garbed men in their long coats and *peyot* (curled sidelocks) and women wearing long-sleeved dresses and black stockings, their heads covered with a scarf or *sheitl* (wig), were rushing along. Brizel's Bakery, in its 8-by 10-foot selling space, was already packed with customers clutching their robust challahs, strudels, *fluden,* and cheese Danish.

Berish Brizel, sixty-three, dressed in an apron and sporting a long beard and *peyot,* found time to talk before he rushed off to study at the yeshiva at 7:30. "Baking and prayer are very compatible," said Mr. Brizel, who had already returned from the dawn prayer, where he goes between dough risings.

He told me that his grandparents came to Palestine at the turn of the century from Raisha, Galicia, today part of southern Poland. Like many wives of religious Jews, his mother worked while his father, a rabbi, studied the Torah. During the British Mandate, from 1917 to 1948, Mrs. Brizel made cheese and butter for Jewish Jerusalemites and the British soldiers and baked challah and pastries for her family at home.

In 1948, during the siege of Jerusalem, when foods had to pass through a barricade, the driver who brought them milk was killed. Being a practical businesswoman with a family to feed, Mrs. Brizel turned her cake-baking hobby into a business. "Everyone in the family helped out," recalled Berish Brizel. "And that is how we learned, including my father. A rich challah has to include eggs. The loaf also has to be brushed twice with an egg wash, allowing the coating to dry between brushings, and then baked in the oven. It is tricky to do that because the challah has already risen. You have to be careful. But by doing this you'll get that beautiful chestnut color."

THE ULTIMATE CHALLAH

FROM BRIZEL'S BAKERY AND JACK WAYNE

This is what I call the ultimate challah. Adapted from Brizel's Bakery in Jerusalem, the bread was perfected with the help of Jack Wayne of West Bloomfield Hills, Michigan, who comes from a long line of bakers in Lodz, Poland, once a center of Jewish customs and traditions. Zingerman's Bake House in Ann Arbor, Michigan, makes a variation of this crusty, chestnut-colored loaf and mail-orders it throughout the United States.

When you are making this challah, be sure to perform the *mitzvah* of setting aside about an ounce of the dough.* You can throw it away, or wrap it in aluminum foil as some religious bakers do and place it in the oven. Some people save all these challah-offerings and burn them right before Passover. Then take another piece of dough, fill it with jam as they did in Eastern Europe, and bake it for the hungry adult or child who, smelling the aroma of fresh bread, can't wait for the Sabbath to begin.

This recipe calls for two kinds of flour. Bread flour includes more gluten, helpful in the braiding. However, if you can find only all-purpose flour, use that. It also calls for ½–¾ cup of sugar, because I like my challah less sweet than many challah eaters, even in my family! If you are going to use just one loaf, perform another *mitzvah*—give away the second. If you are making a month of challahs, as I sometimes do, double the recipe and freeze several just after braiding them. Take them out of the freezer 5 hours before glazing and baking.

1 scant tablespoon (1 package) active dry yeast
1¾ cups lukewarm water
½–¾ cup sugar

---

* Technically, the separation of challah with a blessing, according to the Talmud, refers only to dough using flour that weighs at least 3 pounds 11 ounces. If the flour weighs less than 2 pounds 11 ounces, you do not have to separate the challah at all, and if it weighs more than 2 pounds 11 ounces and less than 3 pounds 11 ounces, you can separate it without a blessing. The challah is usually blessed after the flour, yeast, water, and other ingredients are mixed.

½ cup vegetable oil
5 large eggs
5 cups bread flour
3½ cups unbleached all-purpose flour, approximately
1 tablespoon salt
Poppy or sesame seeds for sprinkling

The dough:
1. In a large bowl, dissolve the yeast in the warm water. Add the sugar and the oil and mix well with a whisk or a wooden spoon. Beat in 4 of the eggs, 1 at a time; then gradually stir in the bread flour, 2 cups of the all-purpose flour, and the salt. When you have a dough that holds together, it is ready for kneading.
2. To knead by hand, place the dough on a lightly floured surface. Knead well, using the heels of your hands to press the dough away and your fingers to bring it back. Continue, turning the dough, for about 10 minutes, or until the dough is smooth and elastic, adding the remaining 1½ cups of all-purpose flour or as needed.

   To knead by machine in an electric mixer fitted with the dough hook, knead for 5 minutes on medium speed, or until smooth. You can also process half the dough at a time in a food processor fitted with the steel blade; process for about 1 minute.
3. After kneading, place all the dough in a large oiled bowl, cover with plastic wrap, and let it rest in a warm place for 1 hour, until almost doubled in size. You can also put the dough in an oven that has been warmed to 150 degrees for a few minutes and then turned off.
4. When the dough is almost doubled in size, remove it from the bowl and punch it down—the rougher you are, the more the dough likes it. Return it to the bowl, cover it again, and let it rise in a warm place for 30 minutes more. Or, if you have to go out, let the dough rise slowly in the refrigerator several hours or overnight and bring it to room temperature when ready to continue.

Braiding and baking the challah:
5. To make a 6-braided challah, take half the dough and form into 6 balls. Roll each ball with your hands into a strand about 14 inches long and

1½ inches wide. Pinch the strands together at one end and then gently spread them into 2 groups of 3. Next, take the outside right strand over 2 to the middle empty space. Then, take the second strand from the left to the far right. Regroup to 3 on each side. Take the outside left strand over 2 to the middle and the second strand from the right over to the far left. Continue this method until all the strands are braided. The key is to always have 3 strands on each side so that you can keep your braid balanced. Make a second loaf the same way. Place the braided loaves in greased 10- by 4-inch loaf pans or on a greased cookie sheet with at least 2 inches in between.

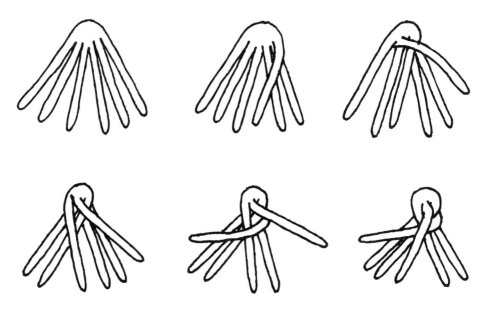

To make loaves symbolizing the 12 shewbread, the consecrated loaves placed on the altar in the Temple of Jerusalem, shape one half of the dough into 12 tight balls and press them together in the bottom of a greased 10- by 4-inch loaf pan. Repeat with the second half of the dough in another pan.

6. Let the challah loaves rise another hour, uncovered. Fifteen minutes before putting the loaves in the oven, beat the remaining egg and brush it gently over them. Five minutes later, lightly brush them again. Then sprinkle with poppy or sesame seeds and let dry a few minutes.

7. Preheat the oven to 400 degrees. Bake the loaves on the middle rack of the oven for 10 minutes. Then reduce the temperature to 375 degrees and bake for 30 minutes more. Turn off the oven and leave the loaves in 5 minutes longer to get a dark-golden crust. Remove and cool on a rack.

Yield: 2 loaves (P)

NOTE: Practice braiding first with Play-Doh, using strands of different colors.

VARIATION: ZINGERMAN'S BAKE HOUSE HOLIDAY TIP

Soak ¾ cup dark raisins and ¼ cup yellow raisins in 6 tablespoons dark rum for 1 hour or more. Add the rum-soaked raisins with any leftover rum to the dough after 5 minutes of kneading, adding a few tablespoons more flour to absorb the liquid. If you are using a mixer or food processor, work the raisins in by hand.

Heavenly Hallah

Andra Tunick Karnofsky

Recently I attended *kiddush* after Sabbath services at Aitz Hayim, a synagogue "Without Walls" located in a community center in Highland Park, Illinois. The lay leader placed a three-pound challah in the middle of the group, where a number of people held it. Then, after he said the blessings, he asked the gathering (about sixty of us) to chant the *motzi*, the traditional prayer over the bread, together while either holding the challah or touching someone who was. The idea is to connect—to provide an unbroken physical and spiritual chain within the group, bridging the secular and the spiritual with joy. We then tore the challah apart, all participating equally, saying, "Raise the challah when you say the blessings. Elevate it."

"People touching each other creates a wonderful connectedness," said Andra Tunick Karnofsky, one of the congregants and the baker of the whole-wheat challah. "By the time we eat, we are physically close together and can continue the spirit of the blessings, the service, and Shabbos."

Andra, a psychologist, has been supplying her synagogue and many local stores with her Heavenly Hallah since 1991. "I always loved cooking," she said. "As the eldest child with a grandmother who was a great cook, the legacy was handed down to me."

Her particular passion for baking challah began fifteen years ago, when her husband, Keith, was a Hillel rabbi at the University of Rhode Island. "We invited students for Shabbos," she said. "It was in the early Eighties, and I wanted my foods to be natural. When I made cookies, I put in whole-wheat grains and wheat germ, so when I made challah, it seemed sad to be serving an all-white bread. I decided to enrich it with whole-wheat flour." Later, in Boston, St. Louis, and Chico, California—wherever the rabbinate took Andra and her husband—she still baked challah and invited people over for the Sabbath. "People liked the challah and encouraged me to sell it," she said. "One of the appeals of baking for me is that it is a transformation. You take a variety of elements in their natural form and you create something completely new and different. It has little grains but becomes part of the greater whole. And so the love you put into the dough is incorporated into the bread."

One special addition to Andra's challah is her team of baker's helpers. As a behavioral specialist at Lambs Farm, a community for retarded adults in Libertyville, Illinois, she contracts with Lambs Farm to make her bread at the farm's bakery on Wednesdays and Fridays with the assistance of from five to fifteen of the adults. "So it's a double *mitzvah*."

HEAVENLY WHOLE-WHEAT CHALLAH

FROM ANDRA TUNICK KARNOFSKY

"When I first started making challah, people either loved it or were offended by the whole wheat," Andra said. "It was supposed to be white." She sees it this way: "My grandmother made white challah, but she didn't have the bleached white flour we just buy in a bag. It had to be sifted; it was expensive, a treat for the Sabbath. Today you buy the flour for the bread and it is white. It takes more effort to incorporate other ingredients, which is what makes whole-wheat challah special today. In our society, it is a reversal because of our American eating habits."

If you like, you can substitute all egg whites for the whole eggs. But then add 1 tablespoon vegetable oil so the bread won't be too dry.

> 1 cup plus 1 teaspoon warm water
> 2 scant tablespoons (2 packages) active dry yeast
> 3½ cups unbleached all-purpose flour
> ½ cup sugar
> 1½ cups whole-wheat flour, preferably stone-ground
> 2 teaspoons salt
> ½ cup (1 stick) unsalted butter or parve margarine, at room
>   temperature
> 3 large eggs
> 2 tablespoons poppy or sesame seeds for sprinkling

The dough:

1. In a large bowl, mix together 1 cup of the water, the yeast, 1 cup of the all-purpose flour, and ¼ cup of the sugar. Set aside for 20–30 minutes—Andra feels that making this "sponge" helps the yeast add an extra tangy flavor to the bread.

2. In the bowl of an electric mixer fitted with the dough hook, place the sponge mixture and 2 more cups of the all-purpose flour, the remaining ¼ cup sugar, the whole-wheat flour, and the salt. Mix well at a low speed.

Gradually add the butter or margarine and 2 of the eggs, 1 at a time. Adding the remaining ½ cup all-purpose flour as needed, gradually increase the speed of the mixer and continue mixing about 10 minutes, until the dough becomes smooth and elastic.

3. Place the dough in a large, lightly oiled bowl and turn so all the sides are coated with oil. Cover with a cloth and let the dough rise 1–2 hours, until doubled in size. You can also refrigerate the dough and let it rise slowly overnight. Punch it down, remove it to a floured board, and knead until the air pockets are pushed out.

Braiding and baking the challah:

4. Divide the dough in half. Set aside one half and divide the other into 4 equal portions. Roll each piece with your hands into an even strand about 15 inches long and place the 4 strands side by side. Pinch the upper ends firmly together to connect them. Beginning from the right and working toward the left, take the outside strand and weave it over the adjacent strand, under the next strand, and over the last strand on the left. Proceed in the same over-under fashion, moving downward row by row, always weaving from right to left, until the ends are reached. Connect the ends by pinching them together as you did in the beginning and tuck them under the braided loaf. Form the second loaf the same way. Place both on a greased cookie sheet 2 inches apart.

5. In a small bowl, beat together the remaining egg with the teaspoon water. Brush the braided loaves with the egg wash.

6. Cover the loaves loosely with a towel or plastic wrap and let them rise for 1 hour more, or until doubled in size.

7. Preheat the oven to 350 degrees. Brush the loaves again with the egg wash and sprinkle with the poppy or sesame seeds.

8. Bake on the middle rack of the oven for 35–45 minutes, or until golden. The loaves are done if they sound hollow when tapped.

Yield: 2 loaves (D or P)

SEASONAL VARIATIONS

Knead the following ingredients into the dough during step 2, after adding the eggs. Owing to the moisture found in some of the ingredients, more flour may be needed.

Thanksgiving and fall: 1 cup frozen cranberries tossed in 2 tablespoons sugar, or 1 cup peeled and diced apples sprinkled with cinnamon sugar.

Winter: 1 cup diced dried apricots or golden raisins plumped in hot water for 10 minutes, then drained and dried.

February, for Washington's Birthday: 1 cup frozen whole Bing cherries, coarsely chopped.

Spring and summer: 1 cup frozen blueberries or diced fresh peaches.

As an optional glaze for challah with fruit, melt ¼ cup apricot jam with 1 tablespoon water. Brush the melted jam mixture over the baked challah.

Ladino Pastries in Zohar's Zulla

Zohar Cohen-Nehemia Halleen

Zohar Cohen-Nehemia Halleen has magnificent recall of childhood recipes and memories. As she nimbly works the dough for Sabbath breads and pastries, she talks about Old Jerusalem. "I learned to make Turkish *boyos,* Yemenite *kubbanah,* and old Spanish *travados* as a young girl," she said. "For fifteen years I made these pastries every Sabbath. They came here when my family did, hundreds of years ago." In her late-nineteenth-century stone house in Rosh Pina is a kitchen overflowing with preserves, olives curing in Dead Sea salt, and the equipment needed by a home baker. Zohar's Zulla (Playroom), as she calls it, is command central for these old recipes. "I love tradition," she told me as we sat around the table. "It gives me roots."

Zohar, forty-one, likes to tell her three young children about her ancestors, who came to Jerusalem from Spain because of the Inquisition. "No one knows exactly when and how my family got here, but they owned a house in the Old City," she said. According to one family story, the first Cohen ancestor came from Andalusia with Omar El Khattab, the second caliph of Islam, who placed the Jews under the "protection" of Islam.

Another story explains how her last name became Cohen-Nehemia. According to Sephardic tradition, for you to be a true Cohen, a descendant of Aaron, the brother of Moses, and a priest in the Temple of Jerusalem, your body must be "complete." "One day a rabbi called my great-great-granddaddy Mordechai Cohen a fake Cohen because in our family we all have a curved-in pinky," she said as she extended her fifth finger with difficulty. "He was insulted about this for the rest of his life. When he died, he suddenly became too heavy and no one could physically lift him up to bury him. The family called the rabbi to examine the body. When the rabbi arrived, my great-great-grandpa suddenly rose from the dead and sat up, looked him straight in the eye, and pressed his second and third fingers and then his fourth and fifth fingers together in the sign of a Cohen. Then he lay down and died. The rabbi was amazed and said, '*Ani Niham* [I ask forgiveness]. Now I know you are a real Cohen.' Ever since, Cohen-Nehemia has been the family name."

Zohar (her name means "splendid" and refers to the mystical medieval commentary on the Bible) grew up in a world of good-luck omens. Garlic strands, "evil eyes," and photos of rabbis still adorn the walls of her parents' home in Jerusalem. Zohar was born in Nahlaot, up to recent times a poor Sephardic neighborhood outside Mahane Yehudah, the Jewish marketplace. Recipes were exchanged in Ladino, the common Spanish-Hebraic language of the neighborhood, and everyone used a communal oven. "No one needed recipes or cookbooks in those days," said Zohar. "They went out in the courtyard, smelled the aromas on Friday afternoons, and learned as I did by helping their mothers."

Even today her baking repertoire is Old Jerusalem Sephardic, with some recipes from neighbors and others brought with her mother's family from Yemen at the turn of the century. *Boyos,* of Bulgarian and Turkish origin, puff pastries stuffed with spinach or potatoes, were eaten on summer Friday nights with a bean soup. *Travados,* melt-in-your-mouth crescent cookies filled with nuts and cinnamon, were served all the time. The Yemenite *kubbanah,* her children's favorite, is an "overnight" Sabbath bread with a hard-boiled egg on top, cooked all night long in a slow oven for Sabbath breakfast.

"When I was a child, the baker would wait until he finished all of his work on Friday," she said. "Then he would put in the Sabbath food, each family having a special towel to cover their dish. On Shabbat morning the women fetched their pans." She still wraps the *kubbanah* in a towel, just as her mother did before putting it in the warm oven overnight. Tradition? Superstition? Maybe both. "The smells are going all over the house," she said. "You want to wake up very early to eat the *kubbanah.* Why do I keep doing it? It gives me sense. It is beautiful." Or, as her mother would say, "*Baruch Hashem, yesh li lechem*" ("Praise be to God I have bread").

YEMENITE KUBBANAH (Sabbath Overnight Bread)

FROM ZOHAR COHEN-NEHEMIA HALLEEN

This is an updated version of the Yemenite Sabbath morning bread, traditionally made with flour and water and cooked in a pot in the embers of a fire overnight. Although special aluminum *kubbanah* pots are sold in Israel, any 6-cup or larger ovenproof casserole with a cover will do.

With the bread, you can bake the Sephardic Sabbath *huevos haminados* for *desayuno* (breakfast). Wrap some hard-boiled eggs, in their shells, in aluminum foil and perch them on top of the pot if possible, or alongside. (Traditionally, the shells are first colored by simmering the eggs in water with coffee grounds or onion peel.) Serve the *kubbanah* with the eggs, cut-up tomatoes, *zhug,* a Yemenite hot sauce, or *hilbe,* a fenugreek mixture. (See my *Jewish Holiday Kitchen,* page 130, or *Jewish Cooking in America,* pages 127–28.)

    1 scant tablespoon (1 package) active dry yeast
    1½ cups plus 2 tablespoons lukewarm water
    1 tablespoon sugar
    4–5 cups bread flour or unbleached all-purpose flour
    1 tablespoon black caraway seeds*
    1 tablespoon salt
    ½ cup (1 stick) unsalted butter or parve margarine
    5 hard-boiled eggs in their shells

1. Mix the yeast in 1½ cups of the water with the sugar. Place 4 cups of the flour in a bowl and make a well in the center. Pour the yeast mixture into the well and sprinkle in the caraway seeds. Using your hands, mix well to incorporate the flour and the seeds.
2. In another bowl, pour the additional 2 tablespoons water. Place the

---

* Black caraway seeds, also called *chernuska,* are members of the pepper family. You can buy them at health food stores or Middle Eastern markets.

dough in the water and let it sit, covered with a damp towel, for 1 hour in a warm place.

3. Punch the dough down and knead it, gradually adding the remaining 1 cup flour and the salt. Here you can cover the dough and refrigerate it until you are ready to complete the final risings and bake the bread. Or let the dough rise once more, covered, for another hour.

4. Preheat the oven to 400 degrees and melt the butter or margarine in a metal *kubbanah* pan or 6-quart casserole fitted with a lid.

5. Punch the dough down one more time and divide it into 4 balls. Place the balls in the casserole side by side, rolling them in the butter to coat them. Cover with the lid and let the dough balls rise another 30 minutes.

6. Bake the bread, covered, for 45 minutes on the lowest rack of the oven. Then lower the oven temperature to 150 degrees.

7. Wrap the hard-boiled eggs in aluminum foil. Place the eggs on top of or alongside the covered *kubbanah* pan and bake overnight, or at least 8 hours. Serve the bread hot, as is or dipped in soup, with diced tomatoes, *zhug,* or *hilbe.*

Yield: 1 **kubbanah** *(D or P)*

NOTE: If you prefer to make 2 *kubbanahs,* just use smaller covered casseroles and divide the dough into 8 pieces.

JERUSALEM BOYOS
(Pastries Stuffed with Potatoes or Spinach)

FROM ZOHAR COHEN-NEHEMIA HALLEEN

The first time I tasted a flaky *boyos,* filled with spinach and served with a hard-boiled egg, I was in the office of the caretaker of an old synagogue in Izmir, Turkey. I was instantly determined to find a recipe for it. A cross between a croissant and a knish, this flaky snail-shaped pastry (using the same dough as in *burekas*) is a Friday night must, served with a white bean soup, in many Bulgarian, Turkish, and other Ladino Jerusalem homes. It is also a Saturday morning breakfast specialty. *Boyos* are definitely a crossover food—my mother-in-law remembers potato knishes shaped like *boyos* from her childhood in Poland.

Make the puff pastry yourself or use a shortcut version with prepared puff pastry.

The puff pastry:
    6 cups unbleached all-purpose flour
    1 tablespoon salt
    1 teaspoon sugar
    3 tablespoons cider vinegar
    ¾ cup vegetable oil
    1½ cups ice water, or as needed
    2 cups (4 sticks) unsalted butter or parve margarine, at room
        temperature
    Vegetable oil, for rolling
    Filling of choice (see below)

1. Place the flour, salt, sugar, vinegar, and oil in a food processor fitted with the steel blade. Then, bit by bit, add the ice water as you are pulsing until the dough forms a ball and, as Zohar says, it "feels as soft as your earlobe."

2. Remove the dough to a lightly greased bowl and let it rest, covered with a towel, for 30 minutes. Divide it into 6 pieces. Roll each piece out on a lightly floured work surface to a rectangle 10 by 6 inches.

3. Gently spread 5⅓ tablespoons (⅔ of a stick) of the butter or margarine on top of each piece of dough. Fold the dough in half from the long side, then fold in half again the other way, so you have a small rectangle about 3 by 5 inches. Repeat this step with the other 5 pieces of dough. Wrap each in plastic wrap and refrigerate overnight.

4. Preheat the oven to 375 degrees and remove 1 piece of the dough from the refrigerator. Using a pastry cutter or a knife, cut the dough into 4 equal pieces. Place 1 piece on a lightly floured board. Roll it as thinly as possible to a rectangle about 10 by 6 inches. Spread one of the fillings over the dough as instructed below. Roll up the filled dough as you would a jelly roll, from the longer side. Take the end of the jelly roll and coil inward with your hands to make a "snail," tucking the end piece under the dough. Repeat with the remaining dough.

5. Place the *boyos* on 2 ungreased baking pans with a rim to catch any excess butter or oil and bake on the middle rack for 25–30 minutes, or until golden brown. Drain them immediately on racks set over the baking pans.

Yield: 24 boyos *(D or P)*

NOTE: You can also make bite-size *boyos*—great for parties. In step 4, divide each piece of dough into 8 pieces instead of 4. Spread each piece with 1½ tablespoons potato or 2 tablespoons spinach filling, and proceed as above.

Potato Filling

4 large potatoes, about 3 pounds, peeled and boiled
1 pound cream cheese
½ cup Bulgarian feta or any hard tangy cheese
2 large eggs
Salt and freshly ground pepper

1. In a bowl, mash the potatoes and add the cream cheese, feta, eggs, and salt and freshly ground pepper to taste. Mix well.
2. Spread 3 heaping tablespoons of the filling over each piece of dough. Roll and bake as above.

Spinach Filling

20 ounces (2 bags) fresh spinach, washed well and dried
4 ounces goat cheese, crumbled
Salt and coarsely ground pepper

1. Remove the stems and chop the spinach as finely as possible—a crucial step for this recipe.
2. Spread 4 heaping tablespoons of the spinach and 1 teaspoon of the cheese over each piece of dough. Sprinkle with salt and pepper to taste and roll and bake as above.

A Teacher of Bakers

Michael London

In Eastern Europe, itinerant bakers used to drive with a horse and buggy to distribute baked bread from the cities to the *shtetls*. Michael London is not exactly an itinerant baker, but this legendary guru earns his living training other professionals to make Old World breads and baked goods. "One of my goals is to rescue the Jewish traditions in baking and to make them available to all," he said as he tossed flour across the tops of unbaked bialys. "Personally, bread goes to the heart of Judaism, because one needs to quiet the mind, to allow the windows of the soul to open to Adonai, God, and other larger forces."

In addition to baking great ryes and challahs, his Rock Hill Bake House near Saratoga Springs, New York, supplies elegant New York restaurants like Lespinasse, Lutèce, Aureole, and Le Bernardin with their artisan breads. He also delivers them to the Union Square Greenmarket. I learned about Michael from Zingerman's Bakery in Ann Arbor, Michigan, one of his fifteen established licensees throughout the country, which includes Whole Foods Markets, the largest natural food store chain in the United States.

Michael, fifty-four, talks about bread in a spiritual, almost mystical way. "We make some of our breads in an ancient manner," he said. "They are made from starter, which we make and replenish without commercial yeast. Dough is a living thing." In a throwback to the religious heave-offering, he takes his best baked loaf of the day and offers it to the fire. "Baking is alchemy," he said. "It's very important for me to be integrating the four elements—earth, air, fire, and water—and to be enlisting the support of the spirit behind them."

Brooklyn born, he grew up with a hit parade of dishes—kugel, *kneidlach*, and such desserts as his Nana's Galicianer prune and nut roll (see pages 145–46 for recipe). Later, in the tumultuous 1960s, Michael, then a literature professor, traded in words for wheat and a whisk. "I was a dislocated, estranged, alienated sort that didn't know what he wanted to do, but didn't want to teach literature any more," he said.

In the early 1970s, he wound up baking bread at Ananda East, a natural food bakery in Greenwich Village, where he developed his Jewish rye bread. On his days off, he and his wife, Wendy, also a baker, visited bakeries. "We followed every bakery that Mimi Sheraton wrote about," he said. "We tasted and tried to duplicate the recipes."

Far ahead of the current bread-baking trend, Michael decided that the best way to really learn was to apprentice with some of the great bakers of New York. "I first went to Mr. Greenberg at William Greenberg, Jr.," he said. "He told me I was completely out of my gourd because I had a master's degree, but I kept on going back to him." Five months later Mr. Greenberg said, "Michael, at four on Wednesday afternoon you have to show up." Although Michael had jury duty that day, he realized this was a pivotal moment in his life. He showed up.

He watched Mr. Greenberg decorate his famous wedding cakes, and learned how to make schnecken from Andrew Martin, a baker who is still at Greenberg's. "Honey helps with the taste and the caramelization," he said. (Mr. Greenberg uses only brown sugar and butter in his.)

After William Greenberg, Jr., Michael worked at Eclair Bakery, the Viennese bakery that was home to refugees after World War II. "At one a.m. on my 'lunch break,' a wonderful Austrian baker, John Richter, taught me how to make the many forms of kuchen, the basics of babka, and how to seal kugelhopfs," he said. "For me, Eclair was a unique opportunity, because I worked on a shift with many Eastern European bakers who were on the verge of retiring." (The original Eclair Bakery closed in 1996.)

Later, when he moved to upstate New York, Michael learned the art of hand-rolled kaiser rolls from Rudy Cohen in Saratoga Springs. The Londons opened their highly successful Mrs. London's Bakeshop there, using many of the tricks learned from the old-timers.

Today, Michael crisscrosses the country, teaching other bakers his techniques. He has certainly made an impact. At the Pittsburgh airport, bearing bags of bread, he was stopped by a flight attendant. She told him that she had just tasted a wonderful challah in Memphis. It was from one of his licensees.

NEW YORK BIALYS

FROM MICHAEL LONDON

"When I was a kid, bagel bakeries made bialys. Bagels spread but bialys didn't," said Michael London during a bialy-baking session. "Once I met a guy driving a taxi whose cousin worked at Kossar's Bialystoker Kuchen on Grand Street. I asked if I could watch the bialy-baking process. The cabbie told me to talk to Tony. I did, and worked that night." Kossar's, one of the last bakeries in this country to make only bialys, is a place I also visited, also at night. What follows is Michael's rendition with my very great approval.

I suspect that, as we know it, the bialy, which means "white" in all Slavic languages, is of American inspiration. I have yet to find a baker born in Poland or Russia who ever heard of a bialy before coming to this country. Canadian bakers and Parisian bakers have never heard of them either, although they both make *pletzel,* like their bagels, with an egg.

The origin of the bialy may forever remain unsolved, but this is my take on it: In Poland and Russia, Jews ate a Bialystoker *tsibele pletzel,* a flat onion bread originally from the city of Bialystok, Poland. It came in two sizes—a larger version, called an "onion board" in this country, and a smaller version, called a *pletzel* (see page 70). My guess is that when immigrants were working in bagel bakeries in New York they made a form of *pletzel* that intrigued their American bosses. "What is it?" one might have asked. "A *pletzel.*" Then the boss would have continued, "*Pletzel,* it sounds too much like 'pretzel.' Where does it come from?" The reply may have been, "Bialystok." The light bulb went on. "That's it! How about 'bialy'?" And so the bialy was born.

Made with the same ingredients as New York bagels—salt, water, yeast, and flour—but in different proportions, a good bialy demands a long, slow rising period. The end result will have a pleasing texture. The center is indented by a thumb and forefinger and filled with diced, sweated onions and sometimes poppy seeds before the bialy is quickly baked in a very hot oven.

1 scant tablespoon (1 package) active dry yeast
1¼ cups cold water

5 cups high-gluten flour or bread flour
4 teaspoons salt
1 tablespoon vegetable oil, preferably safflower
¾ pound onions, peeled and diced
2 teaspoons poppy seeds

1. Dissolve the yeast in the water.
2. Place 4 cups of the flour and 3 teaspoons of the salt in the bowl of an electric mixer fitted with the dough hook. Add the yeast and water to the flour and process for 10–12 minutes, gradually adding the remaining 1 cup flour if the dough is too sticky. (This is a dough that needs to be kneaded a long time.) Put the dough in a large, greased bowl, cover with a cloth, and let it rise for 2 hours.
3. Punch the dough down and scrape it away from the sides of the bowl with a plastic scraper. Cover again with plastic wrap and let it rest for another hour.
4. In a skillet with a cover, heat the oil, add the onions, and sweat them, covered, on low heat for about 20 minutes, or until soft. If you choose, you can microwave the onions in a small bowl, covered with plastic wrap, for 5 minutes. Add the poppy seeds and the remaining 1 teaspoon salt.
5. Divide the dough into 16 pieces and form them into balls, remembering to dust your hands, but not the work surface, with flour. Cover the dough balls with plastic wrap and let them relax for 1 more hour in a warm place. You don't want this dough to dry out. If it does, it will not expand properly in the oven, nor will it color properly.
6. Preheat the oven to 450 degrees.
7. Remove the plastic wrap, flatten the balls, and dust flour over the bialy rounds, using a side swing as if throwing a curve ball. The characteristic of a good bialy is that it is well coated with flour. Place your thumb and forefinger into the center of each to make a depression, not a hole.
8. Place a heaping tablespoon of the onion–poppy-seed mixture in the center of each bialy.
9. Place the bialys on a greased cookie sheet and bake on the middle rack of the oven for 10–15 minutes, or until slightly golden.

Yield: 16 bialys (P)

WILLIAM GREENBERG, JR.'S SCHNECKEN

WITH HELP FROM MICHAEL LONDON

William Greenberg, Jr., master of wedding cakes and schnecken, holds court in his carriage-trade shop at 1100 Madison Avenue in Manhattan. Growing up in the town of Lawrence, Long Island, he learned to bake from his aunt Gertrude. "At thirteen I started selling my cookies to my classmates, and then I graduated to baking for the Five Towns Woman's Exchange, in Cedarhurst. I sold schnecken, cookies, apple turnovers, and mocha tarts. Anything I liked to bake, I sold," he said. Even during a short stint in the army, where he was—what else?—a cook, he has been baking his entire life. Although the family sold the business, Mr. Greenberg still comes into the Madison Avenue shop every day, dons an apron over his hallmark polo shirt, and decorates the special-occasion cakes as he has been making for at least two generations. It was no coincidence that Michael London chose Greenberg's as "the place" to learn about yeast-based baked goods like schnecken. "I owe my jump start to Mr. G. And from Andrew Martin I learned to pin puff pastries and Danish with a rolling pin."

Schnecken ("snail" in German), parent to the American sticky buns, are made from a rich yeast dough sprinkled with raisins and sometimes nuts. That dough is rolled up, then sliced and baked, as at Greenberg's, in butter and brown sugar. By today's standards this recipe is rich—and worth every one of those calories.

The dough:
    1½ cups (3 sticks) salted butter, at room temperature
    ½ cup sugar
    3 large egg yolks
    1 cup sour cream
    3 scant tablespoons (3 packages) active dry yeast
    1½ teaspoons white vinegar
    1 teaspoon vanilla extract
    5½–6 cups unbleached all-purpose flour

The glaze and filling:
   2 cups (4 sticks) salted butter
   5 cups light-brown sugar, loosely packed
   2 cups roughly chopped pecans
   1 tablespoon cinnamon
   2 cups raisins, soaked in warm water a few minutes and drained

The dough:

1. Place the butter and the sugar in an electric mixer fitted with the paddle
    and cream them at a low speed until smooth. Add the egg yolks, 1 at a
    time, then the sour cream, yeast, vinegar, and vanilla, mixing at medium
    speed for about 3 minutes, until well incorporated.
2. Replace the paddle with the dough hook and add the flour gradually,
    mixing at a low speed for about 10 minutes. The dough will be soft and
    slightly sticky. Remove it, dust with flour, and divide into 2 pieces. Press
    each piece into a rectangle about 2 inches thick. Cover each with plastic
    wrap and refrigerate overnight.

The glaze:

3. The next day, cut 2 sticks of the butter into 2-inch pieces and place them
    in a food processor fitted with the steel blade. Add 1¼ cups of the light-
    brown sugar and process until smooth. Remove the mixture to a bowl.
    Repeat with the remaining butter and 1¼ cups more of the sugar. Spoon
    the creamed butter-sugar mixture into the bottoms of 24 3-inch or 48 2-
    inch muffin cups. Using a pastry brush or the back of a spoon, coat the
    inside of the cups completely with the butter mixture. At Greenberg's, a
    pastry bag is used to do this.
4. Scatter the nuts generously over the butter-sugar mixture in the muffin
    cups and pat down gently.

Assembling and baking the schnecken:

5. Remove the dough from the refrigerator. Roll each portion into an 8- by
    13-inch rectangle about ¼ inch thick for the 3-inch cups and ⅛ inch
    thick for the 2-inch cups.
6. Sprinkle each sheet of dough with 1¼ cups light-brown sugar, 1½ tea-
    spoons cinnamon, and 1 cup raisins. Press a rolling pin gently over the
    filling. Roll the dough up carefully and tightly from the long side.

7. Trim the ends of the rolls slightly and cut each into 12 slices, about 1 inch thick for the regular schnecken and ½ inch thick for the mini schnecken. Place in muffin tins, cut side down, so that the swirls are face up. Press them down gently into the tins. Then let the schnecken rise, covered with plastic wrap, for 30 minutes.
8. Preheat the oven to 325 degrees and bake the schnecken on the middle rack until golden, about 40 minutes, resting the tins on top of a cookie sheet in case there are spills. Remove them from the oven and immediately invert them onto waxed paper.

Yield: 24 regular or 48 mini schnecken (D)

VARIATION: A COFFEE CAKE

Greenberg's also makes a sour-cream coffee cake from half the dough: Roll out to a rectangle about 8 by 12 inches, sprinkle with ¾ cup brown sugar and 1 teaspoon cinnamon. Roll up like a large jelly roll from the long side, cut into 3 thick slices, and place each one, seam side up, in a greased 9- by 12-inch baking pan. Bake in a 325-degree oven on the middle rack for about 40 minutes.

"We were glad we had a little bread"

Ben Moskovitz

"The only reason I keep doing what I am doing is I don't want my recipes to die," said Ben Moskovitz, owner and baker of Star Bakery in Oak Park, Michigan. "You have to baby everything. Nothing is just given to you. It's hard work." This spectacled seventy-four-year-old man, wearing a white apron, a white baseball cap, and a wide smile, works in his bakery fourteen hours a day, starting at 5:00 a.m.

For years I had heard about Mr. Moskovitz and his Star Bakery. On several occasions Michigan Congressman Sander Levin brought me (and others, many others!) shopping bags filled with Star Bakery's corn rye (see pages 105–6), babka, and *kichel*. "He's the genuine article," Sandy kept telling me, and he was right.

Born in Apsha, Czechoslovakia (now in Ukraine), a country town of about two hundred Jewish families at the foot of the Carpathian Mountains, Mr. Moskovitz grew up on a farm. In 1939, Apsha was occupied by the Hungarian army under German rule. In 1941, the Nazis took his parents away, and he was sent to work camps in Hungary, where he planted trees, worked in a kitchen, and made bullets. In 1949, the American Jewish Joint Distribution Committee brought him to the United States. This is his story from that long-ago time before the war:

"In Apsha, we were living from the farm. Everybody grew their own stuff. We had land and we lived on it, with horses, a cow or two or three, and stables. Every person had a big garden. Poultry and geese we had. It was a big family with everybody busy. I had five brothers and two sisters. After the war, three brothers and one sister remained. My uncle became a farmer in Argentina and my brother Jack has a big farm in Michigan and likes to cowboy around.

"Because we had two ovens at home in Apsha, we baked for our Jewish neighbors. The big oven had a square opening in the floor in front of it, and you would step down and work that oven. The smaller oven, built on top of it, you could work standing on the regular floor, and it was used twice a week, on Tuesday and Friday. We didn't charge for using our oven on Fridays because we were neighbors and it was our custom.

"The big one was used for matzah and once in a while for holidays. People brought their flour and we charged for the labor. The rabbi supervised.

"We ate chicken once in a while, soup Friday night, and fish when you could catch them. There was a river right in front of the house. We caught mostly white fish, like perch. We had gefilte fish occasionally. At Chanukah time we ate the geese and made *schmaltz*. We had a ball.

"There were no bakeries in town. Sometimes a driver with a horse and buggy went to Solotfina ten kilometers away and picked up bread. It was a rye bread. We didn't have bread like here—99 percent of the Jews made their bread at home. Where we lived there was a water mill where they ground the corn, all the same formula. We ate *malai,* corn bread. It was made from ground corn and worked on the basis of a sour with only corn flour. It was crumbly, sandy, and sour. We ate that all week. *Mamaliga* (Romanian cornmeal mush) was the daily food for breakfast. For many people, *mamaliga* was a substitute for bread. Some people kept it a whole day for all their meals. We bought three kilos of white flour and made challah for Shabbos.

"For Shabbos we had challah until the war. Once in a while we could get white flour. Only the rich ones could afford white bread the whole week. I was poor; sugar at six dollars a kilo was a luxury—we never bought sugar; we couldn't afford that. When you are hungry things are different. We didn't add nothing but I adored the challah, it was so delicious. I know challah is better here. Ours was made from flour, yeast, and water. I never had nothing else. When I came to America I realized it is a different world. There is no comparison."

CHOCOLATE BABKA

FROM BEN MOSKOVITZ

A babka is a high cake, but *babka* is also a word for grandmother in Polish, Russian, and Yiddish. My mother-in-law remembers her mother baking chocolate babka like Mr. Moskovitz's for the Sabbath. "And if there was any left over," she said, "my mother would slice it thin, sprinkle sugar and cinnamon on top, and bake it in the oven for breakfast. We didn't have any toaster ovens then. Now that was a treat!"

When making Star Bakery's babka recipe, I use imported bittersweet chocolate for the filling. I have also given choices to make this recipe parve or dairy. You can make it with high-gluten and cake flour, as Mr. Moskovitz does, or simply use all-purpose flour. However you decide to fill your babka, this is a wonderful recipe.

The cake:
>   1 cup lukewarm milk or water
>   1 scant tablespoon (1 package) active dry yeast
>   4 cups unbleached all-purpose flour
>   1 cup (2 sticks) unsalted butter or parve margarine, at room
>   temperature
>   ⅔ cup sugar
>   1½ teaspoons salt
>   5 large eggs
>   1½ teaspoons vanilla extract
>   1½ cups cake or unbleached all-purpose flour, approximately

The filling and egg wash*
>   ¼ cup unsalted butter or parve margarine
>   ¾ cup apricot jam or ¼ cup almond paste

* See also the apple filling on page 48.

　　1 cup leftover cake or pound-cake crumbs
　　¾ cup chopped almonds (optional)
　　9 ounces good bittersweet chocolate, preferably imported
　　1 large egg, beaten
　　1 tablespoon water

The streusel:
　　3 tablespoons sugar
　　6 tablespoons unbleached all-purpose flour
　　3 tablespoons unsalted butter or parve margarine

The cake:
1. Place the milk or water, yeast, and 2 cups of the high-gluten or all-purpose flour in the bowl of an electric mixer fitted with the paddle. Mix for about 1 minute on low speed until well incorporated. Transfer this "sponge" to another bowl. Cover with a towel and let it sit for 1 hour, until doubled in bulk.
2. Cream the butter or margarine and the sugar in the bowl of the electric mixer. Add the sponge, salt, eggs, and vanilla, and continue mixing at a low speed until incorporated, about 3 minutes. Gradually add the remaining 3½ cups of the flours and work the ingredients for 12–15 minutes on low speed until the dough is smooth, adding more flour as needed. The dough will be soft. Remove the dough from the bowl. Divide it into 3 pieces and dust the pieces with flour. Cover each loosely with plastic wrap and refrigerate overnight.
3. The next day, remove the dough from the refrigerator and let it sit for about 20 minutes while you prepare the filling. Dust a work surface with flour. Shape 1 piece of the dough with your hands into a rough oblong, adding more flour if needed, and roll it out into a rectangle about 8 by 12 inches, ¼ inch thick.

Filling and assembling the babkas:
4. Melt the butter or margarine and place it in a food processor fitted with the steel blade. Add the apricot jam or almond paste and the cake crumbs and process until smooth. Spoon one third of the filling onto one of the dough rectangles and spread it with a spatula, leaving a ½-inch

border all around. Sprinkle with one third of the almonds. Grate the
chocolate in the food processor and sprinkle one third of it over the
dough, leaving the borders. Brush the borders with the egg mixed with
water to help seal the babka.

5. Roll the dough up like a jelly roll from the longer end, close the ends, and
   then gently twist the roll into a spiral. Fit this into a 9- by 5-inch greased
   loaf pan. Fill and roll up the other 2 rectangles of dough and either twist
   them as above and put them in loaf pans or make 1 large babka. To make
   a large babka, link 2 rolls (not twisted) end to end in a circle in a greased
   9- or 10-inch babka or bundt pan, seam side up, and press the ends
   together.

Making the streusel and baking the babkas:

6. Using your fingers, combine the sugar, flour, and butter or margarine and
   sprinkle one third on top of each babka. Let the babkas rise over the tops
   of the pans, about 1 hour.

7. Preheat the oven to 350 degrees.

8. Bake the babkas on the middle rack for 45 minutes, or until the streusel
   is golden brown. Mr. Moskovitz says to press on the dough. If your finger goes in easily, the babka is not done.

Yield: 1 large and 1
small or 3 small
babka loaves
(D or P)

VARIATION: APPLE FILLING

**1 pound flavorful apples, peeled, cored, and coarsely chopped (about
    2 apples)**
2 tablespoons sugar
½ teaspoon cinnamon

1. On a lightly floured board, roll out one third of the dough to a rectangle
    6 by 18 inches. Mix the apples, sugar, and cinnamon in a small bowl.
    Cover half the dough with the apple mixture, leaving bare a rectangle 6
    by 9 inches, and leaving a ½-inch border all around. Brush the border
    with the egg wash. Fold the uncovered half of the dough over the half
    with the apples, pinch the edges to seal, and gently twist the dough along
    the 6-inch side, as you would wring out a towel.
2. Place the dough in a greased 9- by 5-inch loaf pan and proceed as you did
    with the chocolate babka in making the streusel and baking.

KUCHEM-BUCHEM (Cocoa-dipped Babka Rolls)

FROM JEANNIE LAZINSKY

Babka dough can be twisted into all kinds of wonderful shapes. One outrageously delicious variation is *kuchem-buchem,* clusters of babka dough filled and rolled in cocoa and then baked. It comes from Jeannie Lazinsky, a relative of Ann Amernick, who was assistant pastry chef at the White House and a contributor here too (see pages 107–8). *Kuchem-buchem* is one of those marvelous made-up Yiddish rhyming names.

½ cup (1 stick) unsalted butter or parve margarine, at room
    temperature
¼ cup Dutch-process unsweetened cocoa
¾ cup sugar
2 cups babka dough (one third of the babka dough recipe above)

1. Melt the butter or margarine and mix it with the cocoa and sugar.
2. Take the dough from the refrigerator and knead it for about 5 minutes.
3. Divide the dough into 9 pieces and shape them into balls. Take a teaspoon of the cocoa mixture and, using your fingers, press it into the middle of one of the balls, and gently reshape the ball. Repeat with the other balls of dough. Place the remaining cocoa mixture in a wide bowl and roll the balls of dough in it. Then fit them side by side into a greased 8- by 8-inch pan. Cover and let the balls of dough rise in a warm place for about 1½ hours.
4. Preheat the oven to 350 degrees and bake the *kuchem-buchem* on the middle rack for 25–30 minutes, or until firm outside.

Yield: 9 **kuchem-buchem** *(D or P)*

KICHEL (Bow Tie Cookies)

FROM BEN MOSKOVITZ

Kichel, coming from the same root as *kuchen* in Yiddish, means "cookie" and is either sweet or savory. This particular version, rolled in sugar before baking, is very light—it melts in your mouth. "On Saturday night in Apsha, before the war, people had tea and *kichel,*" said Ben Moskovitz while making this recipe.

> 5 large eggs
> ½ teaspoon vanilla extract
> ⅔ cup vegetable oil
> 1 teaspoon sugar, plus 1 cup for rolling
> 2⅓ cups high-gluten or unbleached all-purpose flour
> 1 teaspoon salt

1. Place the eggs, vanilla, vegetable oil, 1 teaspoon sugar, the flour, and salt in the bowl of an electric mixer fitted with the paddle and blend on low speed until incorporated; then beat on high for 5 minutes.
2. Remove the paddle and scrape the batter down the sides of the bowl. Rest the dough in the bowl, covered, until soft and spongy outside, about 1 hour. Then remove it from the bowl—it will be sticky—and make a ball out of it.
3. Preheat the oven to 350 degrees and grease 2 cookie sheets.
4. Sprinkle a work surface with the 1 cup sugar, about ⅛ inch deep. Place the dough in the center, flatten it slightly with a rolling pin, and sprinkle the dough liberally with sugar. "Don't be bashful with the sugar," says Mr. Moskovitz. Roll the dough to a thickness of ⅛ inch, a rectangle about 18 by 12 inches. Then, using a pastry cutter or a dull knife, cut the dough into strips ¾ inch wide and 2 inches long. Lift each strip, twist in the middle to make a bow tie, and place on the cookie sheets, leaving ½ inch between each strip.

5. Bake the *kichel* for 25–30 minutes on the middle rack of the oven, until the cookies are hard to the touch on all corners and golden brown. (If using 1 oven, put the cookie sheets on the top and center racks; then switch them midway). To test for doneness, break a *kichel* in half. If it is doughy or too soft, it is not done yet. Return to the oven for a few minutes more.

Yield: about 70 kichel *(P)*

ROSH
HASHANAH

ZWETSCHGENKUCHEN,
from Lisl Nathan Regensteiner

APRICOT HONEY CAKE,
from Ben Moskovitz

CHOCOLATE LOVERS' HONEY CAKE,
from Andra Tunick Karnofsky

HEAVENLY APPLE CAKE,
from Andra Tunick Karnofsky

CECIARCHIATA TAIGLACH,
from Edda Servi Machlin

PARISIAN PLETZEL,
from Finkelsztajn's

FIG FLUDEN,
from Finkelsztajn's

God said: Let the earth sprout forth with sprouting-growth, plants that seed forth seeds, fruit trees that yield fruit, after their kind, (and) in which is their seed, upon the earth! It was so. The earth brought forth sprouting-growth, plants that seed forth seeds, after their kind, trees that yield fruit, in which is their seed, after their kind. God saw that it was good.

GENESIS 1:11–12

The Rosh Hashanah table is laden with delicacies representing optimism for a sweet future. Dishes abound with honey, raisins, carrots, and apples—all seasonal reminders of hope for the new year. Jews throughout the world bake sweets with honey, *mit lechig* in Yiddish, for this holiday. Because of the harvest season at the period of Rosh Hashanah, it is natural that the symbolic foods were chosen from those fruits and vegetables abundant at that time of the year. Both Sephardic and Ashkenazic Jews say a blessing over challah, as well as an apple, and dip them in honey: "May it be Thy will to renew unto us a good and sweet year." On the second night, another fruit (pomegranate, when available) evokes the blessing: "In the coming year may we be rich and replete with acts inspired by religion and piety as this pomegranate is rich and replete with seeds."

One of my favorite meals of the year is lunch after the first day of Rosh Hashanah. I invite a few close friends and family to a buffet after synagogue. After blessing the round challah for a full year and dipping an apple in honey, we sit down to eat lunch, which I finish with *zwetschgenkuchen* (pages 59–60), honey cake (pages 61–64), and Edda Servi Machlin's version of *taiglach* (pages 68-69), and we linger there for the afternoon.

Bavarian Bugles and Baking

Lisl Nathan Regensteiner

My aunt Lisl grew up toward the end of the German Empire in the Bavarian city of Augsburg. Each morning, in that world that is no more, the postman would get off his horse and sound his French horn to herald the arrival of mail. He often arrived at the same moment that the cook removed from the oven the buttery breakfast schnecken, which we know as sticky buns, one of the hallmarks of southern German baking (see pages 38–40 for recipe).

Lisl Nathan Regensteiner was born into this charming world in 1899 and died ninety-four years later in Rhode Island. She was typical of a particular generation of middle-class European women who came of age between the two world wars. Baking was an integral part of their lives.

Like many middle-class girls at the time in Germany, Lisl and her older sister Trudel learned about baking from a shared Nuremberg miniature kitchen complete with replicas of tube pans and other baking items. It was used by three generations of young cooks—my grandmother, my aunts, and their daughters—as a toy and an educational instrument. Dressed in uniforms with white aprons and bonnets, the young ladies baked miniature fruit and nut kuchen and torten in the copper molds. Today, that kitchen resides in our home in Washington, D.C. A fourth generation, my three children, including my son, have grown up playing with its two hundred pieces.

Besides cooking in the miniature kitchen, my aunt learned to bake breads and butter-rich pastries for the family by watching her mother and grandmother. For the Sabbath her grandmother baked *berches* (the Sabbath bread) from flour, yeast, potatoes, salt, and water. Others, less fortunate, brought their loaves to the baker who, for a small fee, finished them off in his oven, built into the wall in a kitchen attached to his home.

In 1933, when Hitler became chancellor of Germany, the lives of Lisl, her husband, Ludwig, and their three children changed forever. Although Ludwig believed that Nazi rule would only be a passing nightmare, Lisl realized, by 1937, that the time had come to leave. Because my father, her younger brother, had left Germany in 1929 and was already an American citizen, he was able to arrange affidavits for the rest of the family to cross the ocean.

Like other immigrants in America, Lisl found herself using cooking and baking skills to feed at least ten family members, including her parents and her husband's brother and his family, who joined them in 1940. She also helped settle 135 less fortunate refugees. But unlike most refugees, she had had time to bring with her many family possessions, including cooking pots and pans and her grandmother's and mother's heirloom handwritten cookbooks of traditional Bavarian recipes, given to her on her wedding day.

These traditional recipes had come to America a hundred years earlier with the large wave of Bavarian immigrants in the nineteenth century. By the time my aunt arrived, the recipes, translated into English, had already been published and eventually Americanized in *The Joy of Cooking* and *The Settlement Cook Book.* A typical southern German special-occasion dessert like *igel torte,* an icebox cake made from ladyfingers, coffee, and cream with roasted almonds stuck into the cake like porcupine quills, was dubbed Porcupine Icebox Cake in *The Settlement Cook Book* and, in a later edition, Mocha Icebox Cake. As advertisers in America introduced new shortcut and modern methods of baking, these recipes evolved, unlike in Europe, where they often stayed more classically the same.

I remember that when I was a child, Lisl's house often had the sweet smell of baking mixed with the pungent scent of my grandfather's ever-present cigars. Before my aunt even asked, I would cross the breezeway from the kitchen to the garage and open every single cookie tin to see what she had baked since my last visit. Each was filled with a different-color iced butter cookie, sometimes topped with scattered nuts.

I would watch while her fingers deftly shaped the dough into luscious cakes for our family gatherings. Her signature dishes were *gesundheitskuchen,* a simple tea cake (see pages 114–15 for her recipe), and the plum-filled *zwetschgenkuchen,* which she reserved for Rosh Hashanah. "I have made these so many times, I don't even look in the book anymore," she once told me. When friends and relatives complained that they could not duplicate her recipes, she could never understand why.

She said perhaps it was because she used tube and tart pans brought with her from Germany. I always suspected, however, that the real reason for the success of her baking had nothing to do with the pans she used. Her pastries were touched by compassion and love.

ZWETSCHGENKUCHEN
(Southern German and Alsatian Italian Plum Tart)

FROM LISL NATHAN REGENSTEINER

The following southern German and Alsatian *zwetschgenkuchen* is served traditionally at the high holidays in early fall, when the small blue Italian plums are in season. In southern Germany and Alsace the tart was made from *zwetsche* (in French, *quetsche*), a local variety of these plums. My aunt Lisl always used a *mürbeteig* crust (a short-crust butter cookie dough) for this tart, and sliced each Italian plum into four crescent shapes. She lined the tart with breadcrumbs and then apricot preserves, which protected the dough during baking, creating a crispy crust. She went light on the cinnamon, a spice she felt was overused in this country. (I agree with her.) She made an *apfelkuchen* in much the same manner. My aunt's results, simple to prepare, were simply delicious.

1 cup unbleached all-purpose flour
Dash of salt
¼ cup sugar
½ cup (1 stick) unsalted butter or parve margarine
1 large egg yolk
2 teaspoons dried breadcrumbs
⅓ cup apricot preserves
1 tablespoon brandy
2 pounds Italian plums
½ teaspoon cinnamon
Confectioners' sugar

1. To make the crust using a food processor fitted with the metal blade, pulse the flour, salt, and 1 tablespoon of the sugar together. Cut the butter or margarine into small pieces, add to the bowl, and process until crumbly. Add the egg yolk and process until the dough forms a ball, adding more flour if necessary.

To make the dough by hand, use your fingers or a pastry blender to work the butter or parve margarine into the flour, salt, and 1 tablespoon sugar until the mixture resembles coarse breadcrumbs. Add the egg yolk and work the dough into a ball.

2. Remove the dough from the bowl, dust with flour, and pat into a flattened circle. Cover with plastic wrap and refrigerate for at least a half hour.

3. When you are ready to make the crust, dust your hands and the dough with flour. Place the dough in the center of a 9-inch pie plate and with your fingers gently pat it out to cover the bottom and go up the sides. Trim the crust and prick the bottom in several places with the tines of a fork.

4. Preheat the oven to 400 degrees.

5. Prebake the crust on the middle rack for 10 minutes. Remove from the oven and let cool slightly. Turn the oven down to 350 degrees.

6. Pit and cut the plums into fourths. Sprinkle the bread crumbs on the crust, then spoon the apricot preserves on top and drizzle with the brandy. Place the plum quarters on the crust in concentric circles, starting from the outside and working inward, so that each overlaps the next, into the center. Sprinkle with cinnamon and the remaining sugar. (At this point, if you wish, you can wrap and freeze the tart, to bake it later. Just remove it from the freezer one hour before baking.)

7. Place the tart in the oven and bake about 30–40 minutes or until the crust is golden brown and the plums are juicy. Remove from the oven. Just before serving, sprinkle with confectioners' sugar.

Yield: 6–8 servings (D or P)

APRICOT HONEY CAKE

FROM BEN MOSKOVITZ

"One thing I cannot get in my head," said Ben Moskovitz, owner of Star Bakery in Oak Park, Michigan (see pages 43–44). "Was the food better growing up in Czechoslovakia or were the people hungrier there? My mother made a honey cake for the holiday, and it was so delicious. Honey was too expensive for us, so my mother burned the sugar to make it brown. Here I use pure honey, but I still think my mother's cake was better and I know I am wrong. The taste of hers is still in my mouth."

Mr. Moskovitz's European honey cake follows, with a few of my American additions. Other European Jewish bakers interviewed for this book also bake with white rye flour and cake flour when we would use all-purpose flour. I have included both choices.

½ cup dried apricots, roughly chopped
¼ cup dark rum
2 large eggs
1 cup clover honey
⅓ cup vegetable oil
Grated peel and juice of 1 lemon
Grated peel and juice of 1 orange
⅓ cup sugar
1 teaspoon salt
⅓ cup apricot jam
1¾ cups white rye* or unbleached all-purpose flour
¼ cup cake or unbleached all-purpose flour
½ teaspoon baking soda
½ cup slivered almonds, or roughly chopped walnuts or cashews

* White rye flour is available from King Arthur Flour (see page 202), and can be ordered through their *Baker's Catalogue*. Or you may want to ask your local bakery if they will sell you some.

1. In a small bowl, soak the apricots in the rum for at least 30 minutes.
2. Preheat the oven to 350 degrees and grease a 10- by 5-inch loaf pan.
3. In a mixing bowl, beat the eggs with a whisk. Stir in the honey, vegetable oil, grated lemon and orange peel and juice, sugar, salt, and apricot jam.
4. Sift the 2 flours and the baking soda into another bowl.
5. Strain the apricots, reserving the excess rum.
6. Add the flour alternately with the rum to the honey cake mixture. Fold in the apricots. Scoop the batter into the prepared pan and sprinkle with the nuts.
7. Bake on the lower oven rack for 50–55 minutes, or until the center of the cake is firm when you press it. Remove from the oven and cool on a rack.

Yield: 1 cake (P)

CHOCOLATE LOVERS' HONEY CAKE

FROM ANDRA TUNICK KARNOFSKY

This decidedly American chocolate chocolate-chip honey cake is included in the Rosh Hashanah gift packs Andra Karnofsky (see pages 24–25) sends to college students. She uses mini chocolate chips so they won't sink to the bottom.

2 ounces unsweetened chocolate
2 cups unbleached all-purpose flour
½ teaspoon baking soda
1 teaspoon baking powder
1½ teaspoons cinnamon
2 large eggs
3 tablespoons vegetable oil
¾ cup honey
⅔ cup light-brown sugar
½ cup orange juice
1 cup mini chocolate chips

1. Preheat the oven to 350 degrees and grease a 9- by 5-inch loaf pan. Melt the unsweetened chocolate over simmering water in a double boiler or microwave for 1 minute. Set aside.
2. Sift into a mixing bowl the flour, baking soda, baking powder, and cinnamon and set aside.
3. In a larger bowl, beat the eggs and add the oil and honey. Then add the brown sugar and melted chocolate.
4. Alternately add the dry ingredients and the orange juice. Stir in ¾ cup of the chocolate chips.
5. Pour the batter into the loaf pan. Sprinkle the remaining ¼ cup chocolate chips over the top.
6. Bake on the lower rack of the oven for 50–55 minutes, or until a tooth-

pick inserted in the center comes out clean. Cool on a rack for about 15 minutes. Gently run a knife around the edges to loosen the cake, then remove it from the pan.

Yield: 1 cake (P)

HEAVENLY APPLE CAKE

FROM ANDRA TUNICK KARNOFSKY

In my family we always inaugurate the Jewish New Year with our first apple dessert of the fall season. The tradition in Andra's home is to begin the year with a round challah and to end it with a cake topped with concentric circles of sliced apples. This dessert is very similar to Jewish apple cake, a Polish dessert (see my *Jewish Holiday Kitchen,* page 72) that was very popular in church cookbooks throughout Maryland. I believe it is called Jewish because it is an oil-based rather than a butter-based cake. Andra's version is particularly easy, attractive, and delicious.

3 cups unbleached all-purpose flour
2 tablespoons wheat germ (optional)
½ teaspoon salt
1 tablespoon baking powder
6 small Rome, Granny Smith, Yellow Delicious,
    or other low-moisture apples
Juice of ½ lemon
4 large eggs
1 cup vegetable oil
2 cups sugar
1 tablespoon vanilla extract
½ cup orange juice
1 teaspoon cinnamon

1. Preheat the oven to 350 degrees. Grease and flour a 9-inch springform pan.
2. Mix the flour, wheat germ, salt, and baking powder in a bowl and set aside.
3. Peel, core, and slice the apples into eighths and place in another bowl. Sprinkle with lemon juice.

4. In a third bowl, beat the eggs until foamy. Add the vegetable oil and 1¾ cups of the sugar; beat well. Stir in the vanilla.
5. To the egg mixture, alternately add the dry ingredients and the orange juice. Pour half the batter into the prepared pan. Cover with half the sliced apples.
6. In a small bowl, mix the remaining ¼ cup sugar with the cinnamon and sprinkle half over the apples. Cover with the remaining batter.
7. Starting at the outside of the pan, neatly place the remaining apple slices in overlapping concentric circles. Sprinkle with the remaining cinnamon-sugar mixture.
8. Put some aluminum foil on the bottom of the oven in case the batter leaks. Bake the cake on the middle rack for 1¼ hours, or until a toothpick inserted in the center comes out clean. Cool on a rack before you carefully remove the cake from the pan.

Yield: 1 cake (P)

"In our soul, in our heart, we never forgot we were Jews"

Edda Servi Machlin

For years I've admired the work that Edda Servi Machlin, author of the two-volume *Classic Cuisine of the Italian Jews,* has done in bringing to the American public the food and stories of her family in Pitigliano as well as recipes of other Italian Jews. One hot August afternoon I visited her at home in the town of Croton-on-Hudson, New York. For lunch, she served a meal from Volume 2, including a delicious molded fettuccine and *fruste,* a crusty bread that she bakes all the time for her husband, Gene, and their two daughters. Her house, hugging a hill, has a grape arbor on the back deck that annually becomes a *sukkah,* and there is a garden resplendent with zucchini, tomatoes, and all manner of salad greens and fresh herbs.

Baking for Mrs. Machlin is second nature. And so are the memories, exuberantly told. As we ate, we talked about the crucial period in her life between November 1943 and June 1944, when "we ran for our lives." Her parents and younger brother were taken to an Italian concentration camp near Siena. "In our soul, in our heart, the four of us still free—my two older brothers, younger sister, and I—never forgot that we were Jews," she said. "We became beggars, often living with peasants from farm to farm. But whenever the peasants celebrated, we made Jewish delicacies. At every opportunity I cooked. For the first time ever we ate polenta, something my mother had thought of as peasant food. Sometimes we had to knock on doors and people gave us bread and cheese just to send us away."

CECIARCHIATA TAIGLACH

FROM EDDA SERVI MACHLIN

Taiglach (little pieces of fried dough dredged in honey) are eaten for celebratory occasions like Rosh Hashanah, Sukkot, Simchat Torah, Chanukah, Purim, weddings, and births. *Ceciarchiata* means "chickpeas" or "little bits" in Italian. This festive circle of *taiglach* is similar in nature to the French *croquembouche,* although it's a crown, not a mountain. It is a spectacular centerpiece with its clusters of dough and nuts, and is totally addictive.

3 large eggs, slightly beaten
2 cups unbleached all-purpose flour
½ teaspoon salt
1 cup olive or vegetable oil
1 cup honey
½ cup toasted and coarsely chopped hazelnuts (see NOTE)
2 teaspoons grated lemon peel
1 tablespoon lemon juice
1 cup toasted and coarsely chopped almonds (see NOTE)

1. Put the eggs, flour, and salt in a bowl and stir to make a soft dough. Turn out on a floured working surface and knead the dough 1–2 minutes. Shape it into a ball, flatten it with your hands, and sprinkle it lightly with flour.
2. Roll the dough out to a rectangle about ¼ inch thick. With a sharp knife or a pizza cutter, cut into ¼-inch-wide strips and dredge these long strips in flour. Then cut them into chickpea-size bits, and again dredge with flour to prevent them from sticking to each other. Scoop up the bits in a large sifter to remove the excess flour.
3. Heat the oil in a small saucepan or wok and fry a handful of the bits at a time until lightly golden, stirring so they are an even color. Drain on paper towels and cool. You can also bake them, one third at a time, on an

ungreased cookie sheet on the middle rack of a preheated 400-degree oven for 7 minutes.

4. Bring the honey to a boil in a 6-cup heavy casserole and simmer over moderately high heat for 3 minutes. Add all the dough balls, the toasted and chopped hazelnuts, and the lemon peel and juice; cook over lower heat 7 minutes longer, stirring constantly.

5. Spread the toasted almonds over an oiled round serving platter and pour the hot mixture on top. Let it settle for a few minutes. When the mixture is cool enough to be handled, shape it into a circle with the help of a spoon and your moistened hands. Let it cool thoroughly at room temperature. It will harden a little. The *taiglach* can be eaten either by breaking off pieces with your fingers or by cutting it into 2-inch segments.

Yield: 8–12 servings (P)

NOTE: Mrs. Machlin suggests toasting whole hazelnuts and almonds by preheating the oven to 450 degrees and placing the nuts on a cookie sheet on the middle rack. Roast for 4–5 minutes, shaking the pan a couple of times. Watch them carefully, so they don't burn. Allow the nuts to cool for at least 10 minutes before chopping them very briefly in a blender or food processor.

Pletzel and the Rue des Rosiers

Henri Finkelsztajn

For almost eight hundred years, since the Middle Ages, Jews have brought their tastes and traditions with them to the quaint rue des Rosiers, located between the Bastille and the Île Saint-Louis in Paris. Although most families have moved to more affluent districts throughout the city, the Marais (meaning "marsh") remains, to this day, the heart of Jewish Paris.

In this ancient quarter's narrow streets, shops overflow with delicacies from Eastern Europe, France, Israel, and North Africa, representing a microcosm of the dishes of the city's 375,000 Jews.

After the French Revolution, Eastern European Jews fleeing pogroms in Poland and Russia dubbed that neighborhood the *pletzel,* the Yiddish word for "square," an area where Jews congregated. *Pletzel* also refers to a circular Eastern European flat onion bread, often sprinkled with poppy seeds, which is sold in Parisian Jewish bakeries. The *pletzel* is similar to the American bialy (see page 38 for speculation about *pletzel* and bialys).

Today the best *pletzel* in the Marais is baked by Finkelsztajn's at their two locations, 27 rue des Rosiers and 24 rue des Ecouffes. "My parents came from Lodz, Poland, in 1931 and learned baking from my father's brother-in-law, a master baker, who came with him," said Henri Finkelsztajn, the mustachioed patron whose family owns and runs the bakeries. Mr. Finkelsztajn and his son Alain work at the rue des Rosiers store and his wife, Raymonde, seventy, works around the corner at the other branch with their son Sascha and daughter-in-law Florence. Those familiar with American delicatessens and bakeries will find similarities, and some intriguing differences, in the cheesecakes, *fluden,* honey cakes, bagels, *pletzel,* and other delicacies prepared there. Using French ingredients similar to those found in Poland, the bakery's popular cheesecake is made with farmer cheese, not cream cheese. The bagels, often just baked and not boiled, are usually twisted before they are shaped into rings, and they include eggs, as they do in Montreal.

Until World War II, Alsatian Jewish bakers occupied the bakeries of the Marais and were considered then the major Jewish bakers in Paris.

The first owners of Finkelsztajn's, for example, were the Alsatian Harscher family, who opened the shop in 1850 and kept it in the family through World War II, although they, like most French Jews, hid in other parts of France during the war. Most of the shopkeepers who remained in the area were deported to Auschwitz.

Refugees from Poland and Russia, like Icchock and Dwojra Finkelsztajn, took over many of the shops after the war. Eastern European babka replaced the Alsatian kugelhopf, and honey cakes the *zwetschgenkuchen*. The area's food is changing once more. Now the influence of Sephardic Jews is reflected, since more than 60 percent of the Jews in France are from North Africa. Old-time establishments like Finkelsztajn's have had facelifts in the last five years to keep up with the changing population and the renovation of the entire area, as food stores are being replaced by fashion boutiques. "Today the Marais is one of the chic places in Paris," said Henri Finkelsztajn. "Jewish food is intriguing to the French, who are discovering ethnicity."

PARISIAN PLETZEL

FROM FINKELSZTAJN'S

This Parisian version of a Bialystoker *tsibele* (onion) *pletzel,* also called onion *zemmel,* onion *pampalik,* or onion board, is very similar to an Italian *focaccia.* Try this flat bread sprinkled with rosemary, and you will see how very close it is.

1 cup lukewarm water
1 scant tablespoon (1 package) active dry yeast
4–5 cups unbleached all-purpose flour
2 large eggs
¼ cup plus 2 tablespoons vegetable oil
1 scant tablespoon sugar
2 teaspoons salt
½ cup cold water
1 medium onion, diced (about ¾ cup)
2 tablespoons poppy seeds
Kosher salt

1. Mix the water with the yeast in a large glass bowl. Add 4 cups of the flour, the eggs, ¼ cup of the oil, the sugar, and the salt to the yeast mixture. Stir well, then turn the dough out onto a work surface and knead for about 10 minutes, or until smooth, adding more flour if necessary. Let the dough rise, covered with a towel, for 1 hour in a greased bowl. You can also leave the dough in the refrigerator for several hours or overnight.
2. Preheat the oven to 375 degrees and grease 2 cookie sheets.
3. Divide the dough into 8 balls and roll or flatten them into rounds about 5 inches in diameter. Place 4 *pletzel* on each cookie sheet and gently press down the centers. Brush with water and sprinkle each with about 2 tablespoons diced onions leaving a ½-inch border. Drizzle the remaining 2

tablespoons vegetable oil over the onions and sprinkle with the poppy seeds and some kosher salt. Let sit for 15 minutes, uncovered.

4. Bake the *pletzel* for 20 minutes, switching from top to middle rack after 10 minutes, or do them in 2 shifts on the middle rack. Then stick them under the broiler for 1 minute, keeping a sharp eye on them, to brown the onions. If you don't have a broiler, raise the heat to 550 degrees and put each sheet on the top rack for 2 minutes or so.

Yield: 8 **pletzel** *(P)*

FIG FLUDEN

FROM FINKELSZTAJN'S

This is one of those recipes that has pretty much disappeared in the United States, but those who remember it rave about it. A *fluden,* which comes from *fladni* or *fladen,* "flat cake" in German, is just that, a flat, double- or often multilayered flaky pastry filled with poppy seeds, apples and raisins, or cheese. It was originally common to southern Germany and Alsace-Lorraine, later spreading east to Hungary, Romania, and other Eastern European countries. Often flavored with honey, it is eaten in the fall at Rosh Hashanah or Sukkot and is symbolic, like strudel, of an abundant yield. I have tasted apple two-layered *fluden* at Jewish bakeries and restaurants in Paris, Budapest, Tel Aviv, and Vienna, sometimes made with a butter crust, sometimes with an oil-based one. But only in Paris, at Finkelsztajn's Bakery, have I tasted the delicious fig rendition, a French fig bar. (Figs, my father used to tell me, were often eaten in Germany as the new fruit on the second day of Rosh Hashanah.)

This recipe is a perfect example of the constant flux of Jewish foods. Today, with the huge population of Tunisian Jews in Paris, it is no wonder that the Finkelsztajn family spike their fig filling with *bou'ha,* a Jewish Tunisian fig liqueur used for *kiddush,* the blessing over the wine on the Sabbath. You can, of course, use kirsch or any other fruit liqueur instead.

The dough:
  ⅔ cup unsalted butter or parve margarine (or half butter and half
      vegetable shortening), cut into tablespoon-size pieces
  2 cups unbleached all-purpose flour
  ½ teaspoon salt
  ¼ cup ice water

The filling:
  4 cups water
  2 tea bags

Grated peel and juice of 1 lemon
2 cinnamon sticks
3 cups dried figs, stemmed
⅓ cup sugar
2 tablespoons *bou'ha,* or other fruit liqueur
1 large egg, lightly beaten

The dough:

1. Place the butter or margarine (or butter and vegetable shortening), flour, and salt in a food processor fitted with the steel blade. Process until crumbly and gradually add the water, continuing to process until a ball is formed. Wrap the dough in waxed paper and refrigerate for at least 30 minutes.

Filling and baking the *fluden*:

2. Bring the water to a boil, then lower the heat and add the tea bags, the lemon peel and juice, and the cinnamon sticks. Steep for 1–2 minutes and remove the tea bags. Place the figs in the water and poach for about 5 minutes.
3. Drain the figs and the lemon peel, reserving the poaching liquid. Then place the figs, the lemon peel, the sugar, and the liqueur in a food processor fitted with the steel blade. Process but do not purée; you want the figs to have texture. Add a tablespoon or so of poaching liquid if the filling is too dry.
4. Preheat the oven to 400 degrees and grease a 9-inch square pan.
5. Roll out half the dough to a ⅛-inch thickness. Put it in the bottom of the pan (it should not go up the sides), and trim off excess dough. Prick the dough with a fork. Spoon in the fig mixture.
6. Roll out the second half of the dough and cover the fig mixture. Prick a few holes in the top and brush with the egg.
7. Bake the *fluden* for about 25 minutes, or until the crust is golden.
8. When done, cut the *fluden* into 16 squares. It is wonderful served warm, with whipped cream or ice cream. Or you can let it cool and eat it as you would a fig bar.

Yield: 16 squares (D or P)

YOM KIPPUR

MONTREAL BAGELS,
from Fairmount Bagel Bakery

IL BOLLO,
from Edda Servi Machlin

HUNGARIAN KUGELHOPF,
from Alex Lichtman

Mark, on the tenth after this seventh New-Moon, it is the Day of Atonement,
a proclamation of holiness shall there be for you. You are to afflict your selves,
and you are to bring-near a fire-offering to God; any-kind of work you
are not to do on that same day, for it is the Day of Atonement,
to effect-atonement for you before the presence of your God.

LEVITICUS 23:27–28

Every Jew is familiar with the fast of Yom Kippur, the day to humble one's heart in repentance and atone for sins of the past year, to remember the dead, to look toward the life of the coming year. For thousands of years since Moses descended from Mount Sinai, Jews have fasted and devoted themselves to spiritual contemplation on the tenth day of Tishri.

On Yom Kippur it is important to feel hunger pangs, to undergo the difficult task of atonement. Up until recently, the pre–Yom Kippur meal was at noon. In America today, most people eat a substantial but not excessive meal late in the afternoon.

At the end of the meal, each person is supposed to eat a morsel of bread and water as a symbolic sustenance through the "white fast," symbolic of purity. After the meal before the fast, a white cloth is spread over the dining-room table in very traditional homes. On it are placed a Bible, a prayer book, and other sacred books, which are then covered with a white cloth to replace the traditional Sabbath loaves of challah.

Often in the United States today, close friends of the family assemble for the post-fast feast. Usually a dairy meal is served, beginning with coffee and a sweet—sometimes just an apple dipped in honey—followed by herring or some other salty food. From there on, it is up to the imagination of the host. It is becoming more and more traditional here to serve a glorified brunch—with bagels, lox, cream cheese, herring, and a kugel of some sort. Add to it a Hungarian kugelhopf (pages 90–91), a Russian babka (pages 45–47), or fruit-filled strudels (pages 109–10 and 177–81). Moroccan Jews eat their *fijuelas,* a deep-fried sweet oozing with honey (see my *Jewish Holiday Kitchen,* page 136), Syrians and Egyptians a cardamom cake, and Yemenites a ginger cake.

I'll Take Montreal—the Fairmount Bagels

Irwin Shlafman

New Yorkers have always claimed that the Big Apple's water makes their bagels the best in North America. Real bagel mavens know, however, that there is no contest between Manhattan bagels and those Montreal bagels that are baked in wood-fired ovens, in much the same way that the first immigrants made their bagels. And that's what the Fairmount Bagel Bakery does, magnificently.

Isadore Shlafman came to Montreal in 1918 from Kiev, in Ukraine, and he did what his father had done before him—he baked bagels. He opened the very first Montreal bagel bakery in a wooden shack "on the Main" (Boulevard Saint Laurent), next to Schwartz's Deli and a block from Moishe's Restaurant. In those early days, the family tied the bagels on strings of a dozen or so, packed them onto horse-drawn wagons, and delivered them throughout the city, often leaving them strung on customers' doorknobs.

"*Er ligt in der erd un bakt bagel*" ("He lies in the earth and bakes bagels"), Isadore Shlafman used to say, whose oven was built so low that a pit two or three feet deep was dug in front of it for the man working the oven. "My grandfather said that the first thing he did was build a pit in front of the oven, buy a kettle for boiling, a chute for throwing the bagels into, and a rolling table," said Irwin, forty-one, who now runs the business with his sister Rhonda. To this day at the original Fairmount, they slide about fifty bagels at a time into the stone oven on a long pine board. To remove the bagels they use a twelve-foot *shalivka* (a long, thin board) with a knife-like edge, which slides under the bagels and helps toss them into the chute.

"In 1949 my grandparents moved to this very house on Fairmount Street," said Irwin. In the early days the bagel business was a night-time affair, from 5 p.m. to 4 a.m., except Thursday night, which was reserved for challah. "There were only poppy-seed bagels then," said Jacob, Irwin's father, in an interview months before he died.

After World War II, Meyer Lewkowicz, a Holocaust survivor, started working for the Shlafmans, stringing the bagels, hanging them on the rack for the driver, bringing in wood to fuel the ovens.

In 1958, Meyer opened the rival St. Viatur Bagels a few blocks away, owned since his recent death by an Italian family. After the death of Isadore and his wife, Jacob Shlafman closed his family bakery and worked with Meyer for a few years. The abandoned bakery on Fairmount became a Jehovah's Witness center and then a day-care center.

One day in the early 1970s, Irwin drove down Fairmount and noticed a "for sale" sign outside the building. "The next thing I knew we had bought it back for $19,000," said Mona, his mother. "We even found an old bagel in the ashes in the oven." For Irwin, returning to that site was mystical. "It was a calling for me," he said. "I look like my grandfather; my Hebrew name is his; and now I'm a bagel baker."

"Baking bagels is like a telephone chain," said Irwin, pointing to his helpers from Central America, Vietnam, Pakistan, Greece, Grenada, and China, and at the signs in French reading *croustilles de bagels* (bagel chips). "With so many different nationalities and personalities, it is important for one of us to supervise," he said. Today, the bakery supplies Price Club in Montreal as well as a steady stream of walk-in French Canadian customers, the minority of whom are Jewish.

"When we reopened in the early 1970s, a man came in one day with some sesame seeds and asked us to dip some bagels in them," said Irwin. "In those days bagels were dipped in poppy seeds, period." Today sesame-seed bagels are the best-selling variety at Fairmount, with whole-wheat second, cinnamon-raisin third, and poppy-seed fourth. Flavored bagels are just beginning to gain popularity in Montreal.

"The success of our bagels is that they are baked from the heart," said Irwin. "We are trying to bake them the same way they were eighty years ago."

This is the recipe and technique that Irwin learned from his father, Jacob, who learned from his father, Isadore, who learned from his father, the bagel baker from Kiev.

MONTREAL BAGELS

FROM FAIRMOUNT BAGEL BAKERY

Unlike New York's water bagels, Montreal bagels include some egg and are smaller and sweeter, more like the bagels in Krakow, Poland, and in Paris. For some reason, according to Irwin, salt was omitted from Montreal bagels in the 1970s. Montrealers may have gotten used to their saltless bagels, but I have put it back in the following recipe. Although at Fairmount they can roll fifty bagels in five minutes and make forty dozen per hour, this baker's one-and-a-half dozen will do for the beginner.

Fairmount bagels are always made with high-gluten flour, as are most authentic bagels. It gives the dough more flexibility in stretching. But if you can't get it, use all-purpose flour. The bagels will still come out fine. They are great fun to make and delicious just out of the oven, even if it isn't Irwin's wood-fired one.

¼ cup sugar
2 tablespoons malt powder*
1¾ cups warm water
1½ tablespoons (1½ packages) active dry yeast
1 large egg
1 tablespoon salt
1 tablespoon vegetable oil
6–6½ cups high-gluten flour
4 quarts water
2 tablespoons honey
Sesame or poppy seeds

* Malt powder is available at many health food stores, and can be ordered through *The Baker's Catalogue* from King Arthur Flour (see page 202).

1. In an electric mixer fitted with the dough hook, place the sugar, malt powder, and warm water; mix on a low speed until dissolved. Add the yeast and continue mixing. Add the eggs, salt, and vegetable oil, increase the speed, and mix until the eggs are fully incorporated. Add 4 cups of the flour and mix for a minute, adding the remaining flour as needed until the dough is smooth and relatively firm, yet slightly sticky.

2. Place the dough in a greased bowl, grease the top of the dough, and let it rise, covered with a towel, for about 30 minutes. Punch it down, remove to a floured board, and knead it for about 5 minutes. Return it to the bowl and let it rise once more, covered, for another 30 minutes. A good bagel dough will have air holes in it at this point.

3. Punch down the dough once more. Remove it and divide it in 6 pieces. Place a piece of the dough in your left hand and roll it back and forth on a work surface 3 times. Then place your right hand next to your left and continue rolling to make a strip about 30 inches long, ¾ inch in diameter, called in Yiddish the *flechtel.*

4. Lift up 10 inches of the dough with 4 fingers of one hand, not the thumb. Then, using your other hand, separate this strip from the rest of the *flechtel.* Form a circle by encircling the 4 fingers with the 10-inch *flechtel,* and close the bagel by pressing down and forward once or twice on the work surface, on the seam between the 2 ends, pushing it away from you. Toss the bagel onto a wooden board sprinkled with flour. Continue with the remaining length of dough. Don't get discouraged: it takes 4 to 5 weeks, 6 hours a day, to train a bagel maker at Fairmount. Roll out and form bagels from each of the remaining 5 pieces of dough.

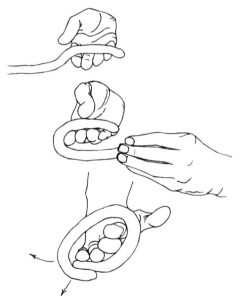

5. Preheat the oven to 400 degrees and grease a cookie sheet.

6. In a large pot, bring the 4 quarts of water to a boil. Add the honey and reduce to a simmer. Slip 4 to 5 bagels in at a time, or the number that

can float at once. Leave them for 1–2 minutes, stirring them so that both sides of the bagel are immersed. The honey gives the bagel a shiny finish.

7. Using a slotted spoon, remove the bagels and drop them onto a cookie sheet. As soon as they are cool enough to handle, dip them into a bowl of sesame or poppy seeds and put them back on the sheet. Repeat the process with the remaining bagels.

8. Bake all the bagels on the top oven rack for 2 minutes. Then flip the bagels and bake for 6 minutes, then flip again and bake for another 7–10 minutes. You must keep your eye on them while they brown. You shouldn't have to bake the bagels for more than 18 minutes total. Remove and eat them as soon as possible.

Yield: about 18–20 bagels (P)

VARIATION: BOZO BAGELS

A bozo bagel is a three-strand, oversized, twisted bagel, a variation I have seen in many Montreal and Toronto bagel bakeries.

1. To make a bozo bagel take 3 of the 10-inch strands, or *flechtels,* created in step 4 above and roll each one out with your hands to lengthen it to about 12 inches long. Place the strands together.

2. Twist the 3 *flechtels* together tightly like rope. Make a ring of them as you do with a regular bagel. Repeat with the remaining dough.

3. Cook and bake as you did for the bagels. Baking time will be slightly longer than for regular bagels.

Yield: 6 bozo bagels

IL BOLLO (A Sephardic Wandering Bread)

FROM EDDA SERVI MACHLIN

I first tasted this flavorful, almost cake-like challah spiked with anise at the home of Moroccan Jews over twenty years ago. Recently, in Paris, I went to a Jewish Moroccan bakery, hoping to taste the bread once again. Alas, this second generation of Moroccan Jews, raised in Paris, had Ashkenazied the bread. They called it Moroccan, but it tasted like traditional European challah and there was no anise flavor.

When I ate Edda Servi Machlin's Italian version featured in her *Classic Cuisine of the Italian Jews,* volume 1, I was surprised how much it tasted like the Moroccan *pain de Shabbat.* "Mine was very close to the original in form and flavor," said Mrs. Machlin. "My ancestors were from Rome and from Spain." In both cases this bread recipe had traveled from Iberia before or during the Inquisition.

Mrs. Machlin serves her anise-flavored *bollo* to break the fast of Yom Kippur and a much more savory *pane del Sabato* for the Sabbath. Others serve *bollo* at Sukkot. Mrs. Machlin serves it with Italian sweet vermouth, her *kiddush* wine. You can shape the bread in the very ancient oblong or form it into a circular snail shape, representing a bird flying to heaven.

6 cups unbleached all-purpose flour, plus more for sprinkling
2 scant tablespoons (2 packages) active dry yeast
1 cup sugar
1 cup warm water
3 large eggs
2 tablespoons anise seeds*
½ cup olive oil
2 teaspoons vanilla extract
2 teaspoons salt

* Anise seeds can be found in health food stores.

1 teaspoon grated lemon peel (optional)
1 large egg yolk

Have all the ingredients at room temperature.

1. In the bowl of an electric mixer fitted with the paddle, place 1½ cups of the flour, the yeast, 1 teaspoon of the sugar, and the water. Beat until you have a very smooth, sticky dough, about 5 minutes. Remove the paddle, lightly sprinkle the top of the dough with flour, cover with a towel, and set aside in a warm place for 1–2 hours, or until doubled in bulk.
2. Punch down the dough, add the eggs and the remaining sugar, and beat again, about 5 minutes.
3. Meanwhile, in a small sauté pan, heat the anise seeds in the olive oil and add them to the dough, while beating. Add the vanilla, salt, and lemon peel. Gradually add enough of the remaining flour to make a soft dough.
4. Sprinkle a generous amount of flour on a work surface. Put the dough on it and knead a few minutes, gathering in flour, until the dough is stiff enough to hold its shape.
5. Divide the dough into 2 equal parts and knead each for 2 minutes; then allow them to rest for 5 minutes. Shape each half into a 12-inch oval loaf and place on a lightly greased and well-floured cookie sheet, or make 2 long strands and coil each one into a snail shape, starting at one end and spiraling it into the center.
6. Cover the loaves with a towel and allow to rise on the cookie sheet in a warm place for 1–2 hours, until doubled in size. (You can refrigerate or freeze the loaves at this point. Allow about 5 hours to bring the frozen dough to room temperature before baking.)
7. When ready to bake, preheat the oven to 450 degrees and brush the tops of the loaves with the egg yolk beaten with 1 teaspoon water. Slide the cookie sheet onto the middle rack of the oven, then immediately lower the heat to 350 degrees. Bake for 30–35 minutes, until the *bollos* are dark brown.

Yield: 2 loaves (P)

NOTE: Mrs. Machlin insists that you use anise seeds in this recipe. "Anise and fennel are two quite different plants," said Mrs. Machlin. "The seeds of the first are used in sweet bakery, the latter in salty dishes."

Mrs. Herbst's Pastries

Alex Lichtman

In 1905, Alexander and Bertha Herbst came to New York on their honeymoon from their native Budapest. Like over two million Jewish immigrants of that period, they decided to stay. Alexander, a cabinet-maker by trade, worked for fifteen years building Steinway pianos, including Toscanini's. On one Yom Kippur, the Steinway Company wanted him to work. A religious Jew, Mr. Herbst refused and quit. From there he started a variety of businesses: he built a newsstand at 79th Street and First Avenue that exists to this day, and he opened a grocery store.

At the beginning of the Depression in 1930, he was fifty-five years old, broke, and jobless. He began a new career out of his kitchen with his wife, known as a fine cook throughout Yorkville, the Hungarian-German neighborhood on the Upper East Side around 86th Street, where the Herbsts lived. Each day at 4 a.m., the Herbsts started stretching and filling strudels with poppy seed, nuts, cherries, apples, or cabbage. "My grandfather built a box that he strapped on his back with a space for trays of strudel," said Cissie Klavens, Mr. Herbst's granddaughter. "He delivered strudel to restaurants by subway until he had enough money for a small truck." (For more about stretching and making strudel, see pages 175–82.)

In 1935, Mrs. Herbst's Bakery, specializing in strudel, *pogacsa,* and *fluden,* opened on Third Avenue between 81st and 82nd Streets, catering to the carriage trade. "I remember the first time we visited Mrs. Herbst's Bakery and I saw chauffeurs coming in to pick up the fancy cakes and pastries," recalled George Greenstein, the author of *Secrets of a Jewish Baker.* "My dad, also a Hungarian baker, took me in the back and I stood there stunned because there were women pulling the strudel. We were all men in our bakery."

Eventually the Herbsts' daughter Elsie started helping out, delivering strudel to restaurants throughout Manhattan, including one where an immigrant from Satmar, Hungary, now Romania, was working. The young man, Alex Lichtman, had worked as a chef and pastry chef at several restaurants in New York City, and had chosen Mrs. Herbst's strudel to serve to his customers. Alex fell in love with Elsie, whom he soon married, and joined her family's promising business.

Until the Lichtmans retired in 1975, Alex did most of the baking and Elsie did the bookkeeping. As in many immigrant families, Alex brought his two brothers, Mano and Louis, to New York in 1938 and then taught them the business. Later they opened Louis Lichtman's Bakery, at 86th Street and Amsterdam Avenue.

Mrs. Herbst's closed in 1986 and Louis Lichtman's in 1987. Upon his retirement in 1980, Alex went to live at West Palm Beach's Century Village, where he taught a course, "Baking for Balabustas [house-wives]." His dream was to write a cookbook, but he died before its completion. "My dad would come up to Newtown for two weeks and be planted in the kitchen, baking up a storm for all my friends," said Cissie. "My father's recipes were all in his head. Many were written down, but we can't find the recipe for his strudel. That may be lost forever."

HUNGARIAN KUGELHOPF

FROM ALEX LICHTMAN

A cross between a brioche and a babka, the kugelhopf (also spelled *gugel-hopf*) was made by Central European and Alsatian Jews. Unlike the classic Alsatian variety, made in an earthenware mold, this Hungarian version does not have candied fruit embedded in the dough. Alex Lichtman shared this recipe with me twenty years ago, when I was writing *The Jewish Holiday Kitchen.* It is a perfect butter-rich cake to break the fast of Yom Kippur and is delicious any time of the year.

1 scant tablespoon (1 package) active dry yeast
⅔ cup warm milk
1 large egg
½ cup sugar
¼ teaspoon salt
½ teaspoon vanilla extract
2 cups unbleached all-purpose flour, or more as needed
½ cup (1 stick) unsalted butter, at room temperature
2 teaspoons unsalted butter, melted
2 teaspoons ground cinnamon
2 tablespoons raisins
1 tablespoon warm water

1. Dissolve the yeast in the milk.
2. In the bowl of an electric mixer fitted with the paddle, mix the egg, ¼ cup of the sugar, the salt, and the vanilla. Add the yeast mixture, then gradually the flour. Beat on low speed for 3 minutes, then turn to high speed until the dough leaves the sides of the bowl.
3. Place the dough in a pan dusted with flour, cover with a towel, and refrigerate for at least 15 minutes. The dough will be sticky. You can leave it for several hours.

4. On a floured board, roll out the dough to a 12- by 8-inch rectangle.

5. Spread all the soft butter over half the dough, measured from the shorter side. Fold the other half of the dough over the butter, sprinkling the board and the top of the dough with flour. Pinch the sides closed. Turn the dough 90 degrees and roll out to a rectangle again; then fold in half again.

6. Wrap the dough in plastic wrap, refrigerate for 15 minutes, and then roll it out and fold it in half twice more. Each time, roll it out in all 4 directions to 12 by 8 inches, turning it 90 degrees.

7. After the second folding, to a rectangle 8 by 6 inches, brush the top of the dough lightly with the melted butter. Cover with freezer paper or plastic wrap. Refrigerate at least 6 hours or overnight.

8. Roll the dough out to a rectangle about 10 by 8 inches. Mix the remaining ¼ cup sugar with the cinnamon and sprinkle on top of the dough, leaving a 1-inch border all around. Then sprinkle the raisins over the sugar. Roll the rectangle up tight, like a jelly roll, from the shorter side.

9. Grease well a 7-inch kugelhopf or 9- by 5-inch loaf pan.

10. Place one end of the roll against the other to form a circle and insert into the kugelhopf pan, seam side up. If using a loaf pan, twist the dough once, holding the ends, so it resembles a bow tie and put it in the pan.

11. Let the kugelhopf rise, covered with a cloth, for at least 1 hour, until the dough is about double in bulk.

12. Preheat the oven to 350 degrees.

13. Brush the top of the kugelhopf with water and bake for 45 minutes, or until the top is golden brown.

Yield: 1 kugelhopf (D)

SUKKOT

SYRIAN KA'AK,
from Mansoura Middle Eastern Pastries

THE SOUR,
from Michael London

PUMPERNICKEL RYE BREAD,
from Michael London

JEWISH CORN RYE,
from Ben Moskovitz

MARYLAND STRUDEL WITH DRIED FRUIT,
from Ann Amernick

SYRIAN BAKLAVA,
from Mansoura Middle Eastern Pastries

GESUNDHEITSKUCHEN,
from Lisl Nathan Regensteiner

Three times a year you are to hold pilgrimage for me, every year.
The Pilgrimage-Festival of matzot *you are to keep: for seven days you are to*
eat matzot, *as I commanded you, at the appointed-time of the New-Moon of*
Ripe-Grain—for in it you went out of Egypt, and no one is to be seen before my
presence empty-handed; and the Pilgrimage-Festival of the Cutting, of the
firstlings of your labor, of what you sow in the field; and the Pilgrimage-
Festival of Ingathering, at the going-out of the year, when you
gather in your labor's (harvest) from the field.

EXODUS 23:14–16

Sukkot, the Feast of the Ingathering, is at its best in Israel. There, after a hot, dry summer that has produced good crops, Sukkot marks, and has always marked, the successful harvest. The main features of the original celebration were the actual reaping of wheat, the gathering of grapes, and the ripening of olives, for which Palestine was famous. Olives are harvested in November, after Sukkot and the first rains.

In ancient times, special ceremonies were performed to induce the first rainfall of the year. One was the waving of branches of the four species of plants and trees that decorate the *sukkah*. They are the palm, the myrtle, the willow, and the citron, which produces a lemon-like fruit called *etrog* in Hebrew.

During the days of harvest, people actually lived in trellis-roofed cabins in the fields. These "booths" were later reinterpreted as a reminder of dwellings that the ancestors of Israel had lived in when they wandered in the wilderness. These booths protected farmers from the strong rays of the midday sun.

To this day, many Jews build a *sukkah* and eat their meals in it for eight days, using wood or canvas and adding branches of trees for the roof, since the sky must show through. Friends help our family decorate the *sukkah*. I ask each guest to bring a decoration and a dish. Together, we dress the *sukkah* with fir branches, dried figs, pomegranates, and grapes—all evocative of the harvest and fall.

A Syrian Jewish Pastry Shop in Brooklyn

Josiane and Alan Mansoura

The sign outside reads "Mansoura Middle Eastern Pastries." In the window there are trays of baklava, nougat, and Turkish delight. Rosh Hashanah is approaching, and this pastry shop on Kings Highway in Brooklyn is at its busiest. Syrian Jewish families like the Mansouras usher in the New Year with delicate pastries sweetened with sugar syrup, along with an array of foods symbolic of hopes for the coming year.

As you enter the door, a bell rings and Josiane Mansoura or her husband, Alan, emerges from the back room where they've been busy making baklava, rolling up *ka'ak,* pretzel-like rings (see pages 98–99), modeling some other Syrian delicacy, or talking on the telephone in Arabic, Hebrew, French, or English. Today the candy made from apricots and rose water is being stuffed with pistachio nuts before being rolled in sugar, and the jam made from Chinese squash is being stirred.

For two generations in this country, the Mansoura family has been catering primarily to the 30,000-strong Syrian Jewish community, most of whom have some family ties in Aleppo, Syria, and now live along Ocean Parkway in Brooklyn. For hundreds of years before that, the Mansouras, first in Aleppo, and then in Heliopolis, a suburb of Cairo, were crafting the same delicacies.

"Both Farouk and Nasser were customers, but still we had to leave Egypt," said Alan, fifty-one, who came to this country in 1961. "King Farouk used to send his limo to buy our Syrian ice cream (made from vanilla, cream, and *sahlab,* a ground orchid root). Nasser, too, came into the store." And no wonder. The Mansouras are proud of their pastries and take the time together, often with their three children, to hand-produce each one. Until twelve years ago, the large table in the back room was used to stretch phyllo dough for baklava and *burekas.* When commercial phyllo became available, Alan's father, now deceased, stopped making it.

On a recent visit we were interrupted several times by Mexican and Panamanian Sephardic Jews placing orders for the Turkish delight and apricot-pistachio candy. Other customers in this Egyptian, Syrian, Lebanese, and Israeli community also dropped in. "You know, even if I had a million dollars," said Josiane, "I wouldn't give up working at this place. I like to see people, I like to talk, and I like to sit in the back room until the doorbell rings."

SYRIAN KA'AK (Pretzel-like Rings)

FROM MANSOURA MIDDLE EASTERN PASTRIES

These crisp, pretzel-like rings—flavored with anise, cumin, black caraway seeds, and *mahlep* (ground cherry-pit centers) and dipped in sesame seeds—are a staple in Syrian Jewish homes. A must to break the fast of Esther, the day before Purim, they are also eaten after Yom Kippur as a sign that a circular year of life has just begun.

Ka'ak and Eastern European onion or poppy-seed *kichel* are considered in Judaism to be "journey cakes," so small that a *motzi,* the blessing of the bread, need not be recited before they are eaten.

Also called *biscochos* (in Spanish) and *crozettes* (in French), these pretzel biscuits are found in every Sephardic community throughout the world. Sometimes flavored with fennel and fenugreek (Iraq), anise (Spain), or coriander (Egypt), these crisp biscuits with a hole, probably the forerunner of bagels, make a perfect snack food or cocktail appetizer.

Josiane Mansoura from Brooklyn's Mansoura Middle Eastern Pastries (see pages 96–97) sometimes adds 2 tablespoons Parmesan cheese to her recipe and shapes the dough into long "bread sticks." She occasionally adds ¼ cup sugar for a sweetened version.

½ cup lukewarm water
1 scant tablespoon (1 envelope) active dry yeast
1½ teaspoons salt
4 cups unbleached all-purpose flour
½ cup (1 stick) parve margarine or vegetable shortening, at room
    temperature
1 tablespoon anise seeds*
¾ teaspoon cumin seeds*
¼ teaspoon black caraway seeds*

* Available at Middle Eastern markets.

¼ teaspoon *mahlep* (ground cherry-pit centers) (optional)*
1 large egg
Sesame seeds for dipping

1. In a small bowl, stir the water and yeast.
2. Put the yeast mixture, salt, flour, and margarine or shortening in a food processor fitted with the steel blade or an electric mixer fitted with the dough hook. Process or mix until a soft dough is formed, about 1 minute for the food processor, 5 minutes for the mixer.
3. Grind the anise, cumin, and black caraway seeds, plus the *mahlep* if using it, in a coffee grinder used for spices until well mixed, but not pulverized. (Or use a mortar and pestle.) Then add to the dough.
4. Place the dough in an oiled bowl, cover it loosely with plastic wrap, and leave in a warm place to rise for 30 minutes.
5. Preheat the oven to 350 degrees.
6. Divide the dough into 38 small balls, a little less than walnut size. Then roll each ball with your palms, against a board, into a pencil-thin, snake-like piece about 10 inches long and ½ inch wide. The dough should feel like modeling clay. Cut into 5-inch lengths and connect the two ends of each length to make a ring with a wide hole.
7. Break the egg into a wide bowl and beat well. Place the sesame seeds in another bowl. Dip the whole *ka'ak* first in the egg and then the sesame seeds. Place on a lightly greased cookie sheet. Make all the *ka'ak,* then bake in batches on the middle rack of the oven 20–30 minutes, or until light brown and firm. Or use 2 cookie sheets and bake on the middle and lower racks, switching about 12 minutes into the baking.

Yield: 76 ka'ak *(P)*

ka'ak and **kichel** (for *kichel* recipe, see pages 50–51)

The Sour and the Mash, Ryes and Pumpernickels

"In Poland we didn't have the white flour you have in the United States. We had a combination of flours. When I close my eyes, I see so many kinds of bread—rye bread, rolls, kaiser rolls, *razovanna* bread (a whole-grain health bread), round loaves of rye and pumpernickel bread with cracked grain, two kilos of wonderful bread, four-pounders that would last for three days and not get stale. The bread we baked back then was fantastic. We had black bread, too, but it wasn't like the Russian bread, more like the rye but darkened with molasses or coffee." So says Jack Wayne, son of a baker from Lodz, Poland, remembering his youth there. Mr. Wayne started baking in his parents' bakery at the age of six. He considers Zingerman's rye pumpernickel in Ann Arbor, Michigan, made with master baker Michael London's formula, the closest to what he grew up with in Lodz. (For more on Michael, see pages 36–37.)

As Michael told me during a baking session, the trick to making a good pumpernickel is in the sour and in the wet mash of leftover rye bread that goes into the bread. On New York's Lower East Side, before refrigerators, Jewish bakers left their moistened day-old bread in pickle barrels covered with cheesecloth and their sours in wooden proofing troughs. "The problem is, the mash molds easily," said Michael. "It was against the law in those days to use old soaked ryes." Had a health inspector seen the soaking bread, he would have made them throw it out.

THE SOUR

FROM MICHAEL LONDON

A good sour, a fermentation of flour and water caused by wild yeasts in the air, should be almost as stiff as the dough. "It should almost be like cement," said Michael. "It has a good smell, which builds up. The trick is to build it up successively until it cracks. I like to sprinkle rye flour on top when I start. When the flour cracks, I know it is ready. It can take from 18 hours to a day. There is a fine line between fermentation and putrefaction."

2 medium onions, coarsely chopped
1 tablespoon caraway seeds
1 scant tablespoon (1 package) active dry yeast
4 cups water
5 cups medium rye flour, plus 1 tablespoon for sprinkling*
Cheesecloth

1. Tie the onions and caraway seeds in a knotted cheesecloth bag.
2. Dissolve the yeast in 3½ cups of the water in a small bowl and pour it over 4 cups of the flour in a large bowl. Stir to mix until it attains the consistency of wet cement. Submerge the cheesecloth bag of chopped onions and caraway seeds down into the center of what will become "the sour." Sprinkle the tablespoon of rye flour over the surface. Cover loosely with plastic wrap and set aside overnight, unrefrigerated. The sour needs air to breathe, but not too much, or it will dry out.
3. The next day, remove the onion-caraway bag and discard. The sour should smell somewhat acidic but not rotten after about 15 hours. At this point feed it (mix it) with 1 cup flour and ½ cup water, or enough to maintain the thick consistency. Cover again and let the sour sit until the

* Available at many supermarkets or by mail order from King Arthur Flour's *Baker's Catalogue* (see page 202).

area between "cracks" in the dough spreads. You want to capture as much of its strength as possible.

4. After it rises again, in about 4 hours, you will have about 6 cups. You can begin to use it or continue to build it up (which increases the amount of sour). Use it in the bread now or refrigerate it. You should feed the sour once every 24 hours with at least 1 cup flour and ½ cup water. The sour can stay several days in the refrigerator without being fed, but, as Michael says, never take a sour for granted. It needs to be nourished.

Yield: 6 cups sour

PUMPERNICKEL RYE BREAD

FROM MICHAEL LONDON

Sukkot is the time to start making pumpernickel. It's a great cold-weather bread, wonderful slathered with butter and served with good hot soup. Once you have mastered the sour, this bread is easy to prepare. Note that with this pumpernickel rye and the following Jewish corn bread you need very little yeast—the sour is the leavening agent.

I love making this bread, but if you'd rather, you can mail-order it from Zingerman's Bake House.

5 slices day-old rye bread, crusts removed (about 2½ cups)
3 cups water
2 cups sour (page 101)
4 teaspoons blackstrap molasses or caramel coloring*
2 tablespoons sea salt
2 tablespoons coarsely ground caraway seeds (optional)
1 cup cracked rye or pumpernickel flour,[†] plus additional for sprinkling
8 cups good bread flour, and more as needed
1 scant tablespoon (1 package) active dry yeast

1. In a bowl, crumble the day-old rye bread into 1 cup of the water until the water is absorbed. Crumble it with your hands; this is what the old-time bakers did. It carries the character of yesterday's bread to today. Remove excess water.

2. In the bowl of an electric mixer fitted with the dough hook, put the rye-bread mixture, the remaining 2 cups water, 2 cups of the sour, and the molasses or caramel color. Stir together at low speed until mixed, about 1 minute.

---

* According to Michael, old-time bakers burned sugar to make the caramel coloring that gives New York pumpernickel rye its characteristic taste.
† Available through *The Baker's Catalogue* from King Arthur Flour (page 202) or at health food stores.

3. Add the sea salt and caraway seeds. Gradually add the cracked rye or pumpernickel flour and the bread flour. Sprinkle the yeast in and stir about 5 minutes, until well incorporated, scraping down the sides of the bowl. Knead by hand for a few minutes. Place in a greased bowl and cover, letting the dough rise 1–1½ hours, until doubled in volume.

4. Punch the dough down, and if it is still sticky, incorporate more flour as needed. Divide the dough in half, gently form 2 round or oblong loaves, and let them rest 10–15 minutes on a floured work surface. Remove the loaves to a floured cookie sheet, cover very loosely with plastic wrap, and let them rise for another 1½ hours, until doubled in bulk.

5. Preheat the oven to 400 degrees, set a rack in the middle, and put 6 ice cubes in a pan on the floor of the oven.

6. Since rye and pumpernickel love steam, brush or spray the loaves with water. Sprinkle some of the rye flour on top and then, with a single-edged razor or very sharp knife, make 5 cuts in each loaf, shorter ones on the outside, longer in the center. Bake the loaves for 45–50 minutes, or until they sound hollow when tapped with a spatula. To keep a shine, brush them afterward with water or with ½ cup water and ½ teaspoon of cornstarch.

Yield: two 2½-pound loaves (P)

JEWISH CORN RYE

FROM BEN MOSKOVITZ

"As every good baker knows, you can't rush. Each dough has its own character and some are more temperamental than others. If you wind up with a stiff sweet dough, you've probably used cold eggs. Let the dough warm up and it will be pliable again. Also, with a sour starter, it has to be babied constantly. The sour is the flavor. Corned beef has to be pickled and bread has to be babied. Make it simple and it will be delicious." That's the point, from Ben Moskovitz, owner of Star Bakery (see pages 43–44).

I have always wondered why American Jews call a very heavy and sour rye bread "corn bread." Somehow, the translation got garbled. In Yiddish, corn changed in meaning from "particle" to "small seed" and specifically "grain," so a corn bread could be any bread made with grain. Some say that the bread got its name because cornmeal is thrown on the baking sheet when it is baked.

Once you have made your sour, baking this corn rye is easy. Make one loaf with caraway seeds (for a stronger flavor) and one without. See which you prefer.

> 3 cups sour (page 101)
> 7 cups bread flour
> 2¼ cups water
> 1 teaspoon active dry yeast
> 1½ tablespoons salt
> 2 tablespoons caraway seeds
> Cornmeal for dusting

1. Place the sour in a large mixing bowl. Add 1¾ cups of the bread flour and ½ cup of the water to keep it wet. Mix and stir down the sides to keep them clean. Cover loosely with plastic wrap and let the mixture sit for 1 hour.

2. Scoop the mixture into the bowl of an electric mixer fitted with the dough hook. Sprinkle the yeast with the remaining 1¾ cups of water into the bowl. Then gradually add the remaining flour and the salt as you knead the dough at medium speed, about 5 minutes. If the dough is too stiff, add more water. When the dough no longer sticks to the mixer, it is ready. Remove the dough, pat it into a round, and let it rise on a floured work surface for 20 minutes, uncovered.

3. Punch the dough down and divide it in half. Add caraway seeds to one half, and form both into balls or oblongs. Let them rise 1 more hour on a cookie sheet dusted with flour.

4. Preheat the oven to 400 degrees. You will know when the dough is ready to bake because its texture softens—it becomes soft like a balloon, and when you push on it with your finger, it springs back and does not leave a mark. Slash the loaves ⅛ inch deep a few times with a straight razor or very sharp knife. Put 5 ice cubes in a pan on the floor of the oven. Before you put the loaves in the oven, brush them with water.

5. Bake the loaves on the middle rack of the oven for 40–50 minutes, or until they sound hollow when you tap them on the top. When you remove the loaves, brush with water, or with ½ cup water and ½ teaspoon of cornstarch, if you want a shinier loaf.

Yield: two 2½-pound loaves (P)

"My daughter, the Jewish pastry chef"

Ann Amernick

Ann Amernick, the assistant pastry chef for Presidents Carter and Reagan, is like that cousin you haven't seen for years yet you can start talking with right away. And no wonder. She comes from a warm Russian Jewish family that values a sense of humor. Her mother Helen Silverberg, her aunt Bea Goldberg, and her sister Abby Lazinsky, all of whom live in Baltimore, travel fifty miles to Ann's home in Chevy Chase, Maryland, every Wednesday to help paint gum-paste leaves, buds, and flowers onto the special-occasion cakes she bakes. Their payment is pride in a daughter, niece, and sister who was the first Jewish female assistant pastry chef in the White House.

"When my mother started out, her buds were terrible," said Ann. "Now she's the bud expert. Every time one of my cakes is in a photo or a magazine, she rushes to see the buds. She no longer cares about the text about me."

Wednesday is the day to catch up on family history and old stories. One of Ann's favorites is about the time the kitchen was made kosher for the late Menahem Begin, then prime minister of Israel. It's a favorite of mine, too, so I'm repeating the story, which first appeared in *Jewish Cooking in America*. As Ann tells it: "For some reason the kosher caterer the White House wanted to use was not acceptable, so at the last minute the entire White House kitchen had to be kashered. I arrived early that day and came into the kitchen and saw three tiny *mashgichim* [kosher inspectors], shorter than I am, less than five feet, holding blowtorches as big as they were. They spent the entire day wandering around the kitchen burning and covering surfaces with aluminum foil. The kitchen was terribly hot with the activity between kashering and cooking. Roland Mesnier, the pastry chef, was desperately trying to get the sorbets made and one of the *mashgichim* was following him around with the blowtorch. Every time Roland turned around, the *mashgichim* were there. While some of the cooks had a partial understanding of *kashrut* from past experience in hotels and lessons in cooking school, the reality in the White House was another story. I felt it was a historic moment, and at the same time it was comical."

Ms. Amernick, a self-taught pastry chef, started out as a child in Baltimore watching her mother cook. "My mother made great blintzes," she said. "From her I learned the way to pour the tiniest bit of mixture in the pan, roll it around, and pour off the excess; so later I felt totally competent making crêpes." As a child, Ann was always fascinated with food. "I would go down into our knotty-pine basement with the wet bar and act as a waitress for my sister and brother. I would bring them little tiny dishes and little tiny cups of ginger ale. I loved doing it."

Then, as a mother, she started baking cakes and has never stopped. From the White House she went to work at Jean-Louis at the Watergate and is now at Cashion's Eat Place. Her specialties are rich cakes and pastries. I purposely had dairy bat mitzvah meals for both my daughters so the dessert would be one of Ann's cakes decorated with pastiches of their interests.

MARYLAND STRUDEL WITH DRIED FRUIT

FROM ANN AMERNICK

"In this recipe I used my aunt Molly's strudel as a base. It was more of a mock sour cream–based strudel, like the one in Marian Burros's *Elegant but Easy Cookbook*," said Ann. "I think it's much easier to work than regular strudel." She also thinks this filled strudel tastes better after it's been baked and frozen or even just refrigerated a day or two. "Then the flavors of the raisins, nuts, and jam have a chance to age, like a fruitcake." Her strudel is filled with the kinds of nuts and dried fruits that are hung, and eaten, in a *sukkah*—raisins, walnuts, and dried cranberries or cherries.

Strudel is the Central and Eastern European Jewish dressed-up dessert par excellence. It was eaten on every possible celebratory occasion, stuffed with dried fruit or apples at Sukkot, cabbage at Chanukah, cheese at Shavuot, and cherries in the summer. Sometimes the dough was rolled, as in this recipe, and sometimes it was stretched. (For more on strudel, see pages 175–82.)

The dough:
  1 cup (2 sticks) unsalted butter
  2 cups plus 1 tablespoon unbleached all-purpose flour
  1 cup sour cream
  1 tablespoon sugar

The filling:
  1½ cups golden raisins
  1½ cups dark raisins
  3½ cups finely chopped walnuts
  1 cup sweetened dried cranberries or cherries
  24 ounces apricot preserves, puréed in a food processor or blender
  4 teaspoons ground cinnamon

The dough:
1. Using an electric mixer fitted with the paddle, mix the butter, flour, sour cream, and sugar on the lowest speed, until well blended. The dough will be very soft.
2. Divide the dough into 4 balls, cover each with plastic wrap, and refrigerate for 3 hours or overnight.

Filling and assembling the strudel:
3. Preheat the oven to 325 degrees.
4. When the dough is ready to roll, mix the raisins, walnuts, and cranberries or cherries in a small bowl and set aside.
5. Remove the dough from the refrigerator 1 piece at a time, and knead briefly. With a floured rolling pin, roll out each dough piece into a 9- by 12-inch rectangle.
6. Spread one fourth of the puréed preserves over the top of the dough, leaving a ½-inch border all around. Sprinkle with one fourth of the fruit-nut mixture. Dust with 1 teaspoon of the cinnamon. Roll the dough up from the long edge for 1 turn. Fold the edges in and continue rolling. Place the roll, seam side down, on a parchment-lined baking sheet. Fill and roll the remaining 3 pieces of dough.
7. Bake the strudels on the middle rack of the oven for 45 minutes, or until golden brown. As soon as they come out of the oven, score them at 1-inch intervals with a serrated knife, then cut 1-inch slices with a regular knife. It is important to cut the strudel while still hot; otherwise the dough will crumble completely. After the strudels cool, you can freeze them, tightly wrapped.

Yield: 4 strudels, about 40 pieces (D)

SYRIAN BAKLAVA

FROM MANSOURA MIDDLE EASTERN PASTRIES

Baklava is to Jews of Syrian and Middle Eastern descent what strudel is to those of Central European origins. However, the technique of making the phyllo dough for baklava is quite different from that of making dough for strudel. Unlike strudel dough, made from melted butter or oil, flour, water, and egg, phyllo is made from flour, water, and occasionally an egg. "We mixed the flour and water and let the dough set for two hours," said Alan Mansoura, the last of eight generations to make phyllo (see pages 96–97 for the introduction to this family of Syrian Jewish bakers). "First we sprinkled cornstarch on a huge table, rolled out a ball of dough on top, then sprinkled the dough again with cornstarch. We repeated this process for about twenty-four layers, rolling each ball of dough on top of the one before, and separating each with the cornstarch. When the dough got wider than the rolling pin we switched to a stick about six feet long—a broom handle is great for this—and an inch and a half in diameter." Alan and his father slowly rolled the dough out paper-thin, until it was five feet in diameter, the entire process taking about an hour. "We would transfer the leaves of dough and cover them with a moist cloth. Then we would use the dough as we needed it."

"Baklava is served at every celebratory function imaginable," said Josiane Mansoura. "It ensures tradition." Since phyllo is now made commercially, however, the family has forgone that arduous part of the tradition.

This recipe, with a sugar–rose water syrup, is lighter and less sweet than those made with honey. The baklava can be frozen before baking. The Mansouras put bright green pistachios from Afghanistan in their version; you can substitute walnuts. If you are using a food processor to chop the nuts, do not pulverize them—they should be chopped roughly to retain their texture.

1 pound prepared phyllo dough (approximately 20 sheets, 14 by 18 inches) FOOD 4 LESS ✓
3½ cups coarsely chopped walnuts or pistachio nuts

※

1 teaspoon ground cinnamon, if using walnuts
1 cup (2 sticks) unsalted butter or parve margarine, melted
2 cups sugar
1 cup water
1 cinnamon stick
1 teaspoon rose water (optional)*

1. Carefully remove the phyllo from its plastic container and unroll. You will have about 20 rectangular sheets. Cover the sheets with a towel.
2. Preheat the oven to 350 degrees. Cut 2 pieces of phyllo to the exact size of a 9-inch round or a 9- by 12-inch rectangular pan. Set these sheets aside, covered with a damp cloth.
3. If you wish to use walnuts, mix the nuts and cinnamon in a small bowl and set aside.
4. Using a large brush, paint the bottom of the pan with some of the melted butter or margarine. Cut each of the remaining sheets of phyllo in half horizontally. Layer one fourth of these sheets into the bottom of the pan, brushing melted butter or margarine over the top layer and pressing down any that overlap the pan. Again, layer with another quarter of the sheets, brush again with the melted butter or margarine, and press down any sheets that overlap.
5. Sprinkle all the nut mixture evenly over the phyllo, pressing down gently with your fingers. Layer on the third quarter of the phyllo sheets, brushing generously with the butter or margarine; layer the remaining quarter on top and brush again. Then trim away the overhang with scissors or a sharp knife. Finally, take the reserved 2 phyllo sheets, place them on top of the baklava, and press down gently with the flat side of a large knife. Brush the top phyllo sheets with melted butter or margarine.
6. With a long, sharp knife, cut across the baklava on a diagonal every 1½ inches, placing your thumb and second finger gently

*Obtainable at Middle Eastern markets.

on the dough to hold it down; then cut diagonally in the opposite direction to make diamond shapes. Brush the top again with the remaining melted butter or margarine.

7. Bake the baklava on the middle rack of the oven for 45 minutes to 1 hour, or until golden brown.

8. Meanwhile, put the sugar, water, cinnamon stick, and rose water in a small saucepan. Bring to a boil, reduce the heat, and simmer gently for 30 minutes, or until the mixture coats the back of a spoon.

9. Remove the cinnamon stick and pour the warm syrup over the baked baklava. Let it stand for several hours or overnight, covered with plastic wrap.

Yield: 24 servings (D or P)

GESUNDHEITSKUCHEN
(Southern German "Good Health Cake")

FROM LISL NATHAN REGENSTEINER

This popular southern German cake, which could be called in English "Don't Sneeze Cake," was my aunt Lisl's signature dish. Baked in a family-heirloom bundt pan brought with her from Germany, the cake was served during *shiva* but also for birthdays, for tea, and at celebrations of the birth of children. Easily prepared, it was the kind of cake that could be made quickly for unexpected guests. In the late nineteenth century in this country, baking powder lightened the cake. Soon poppy seeds and even chocolate chips were added. It is a simple, soothing cake, one that gets gobbled up in my house. This is Lisl's version, with some of my American embellishments.

6 large eggs, separated
1 cup sugar
1½ sticks unsalted butter or parve margarine, melted and cooled
1 teaspoon vanilla
Grated peel and juice of 1 lemon
1 cup milk
2½ cups unbleached all-purpose flour
2 teaspoons baking powder
½ teaspoon salt
⅓ cup poppy seeds (optional)
6 ounces chocolate chips (optional)
Confectioners' sugar

1. Preheat the oven to 350 degrees. Grease and lightly flour a bundt pan or two 9- by 5- by 4-inch loaf pans.
2. In the bowl of an electric mixer fitted with the whisk, beat the egg yolks well with the sugar. Add the cooled butter (minus any milky residue), the vanilla, lemon peel and juice, and milk.

3. Gradually add the flour, baking powder, and salt as you beat at low speed. When the batter is smooth, turn off the mixer.
4. In a separate bowl, beat the egg whites until stiff but not dry; fold them gently into the yolk mixture, sprinkling in the poppy seeds and chocolate chips.
5. Pour the batter into the greased pan or pans and bake on the middle rack of the oven for 45 minutes, or until a toothpick inserted into the center comes out clean. Cool in the pan for 10 minutes, then turn the cake out and cool completely on a rack. Sprinkle the top with confectioners' sugar just before serving.

Yield: 1 large or 2 small cakes, 8–10 servings (D)

CHANUKAH

MEXICAN BANANA CAKE,
from Lisette Span

CLASSIC RUGELACH,
from Ann Amernick

HUNGARIAN DOBOS TORTE,
from Alex Lichtman

CRANBERRY-WALNUT TART,
from Andra Tunick Karnofsky

ISRAELI SUFGANIYOT,
from Brizel's Bakery

Now upon the same day that the strangers profaned the temple,
on the very same day it was cleansed again, even the five and twentieth day of
the same month, which is Kislev. And they kept eight days with gladness, as in the
feast of the tabernacles, remembering that not long afore they had held the feast of
the tabernacles, when as they wandered in the mountains and dens like beasts.
Therefore they bare branches, and fair boughs, and palms also, and sang
psalms unto him that had given them good success in cleansing his place.
They ordained also by a common statute and decree, That every year
those days should be kept of the whole nations of the Jews.

2 MACCABEES 10:5–8

J ews throughout the world light the first Chanukah candle on the 25th of Kislev in the Jewish calendar. The holiday commemorates the Maccabean victory over Antiochus of Syria some twenty-one centuries ago. Going to cleanse and rededicate the Temple, the Maccabees found only enough sacred oil to light the menorah for one day. But a miracle supposedly occurred, and the one day's supply lasted eight. For each of the eight nights of Chanukah, therefore, an additional candle is inserted in the menorah, from right to left, and lit by the *shammash* (helper), from left to right, until the entire menorah is aglow. After the candle ceremony, it is traditional to sing songs, play with the *dreidel* (spinning top), open presents, and eat *latkes* (pancakes) and other fried foods.

The oil used for this frying relates, of course, to the end of the olive pressing at this time of year. Chanukah is replete with desserts fried in or made with oil. Greek women claim that their *loukomades*—deep-fried puffs dipped in honey or sprinkled with powdered sugar—resemble the cakes the Maccabees ate, while Persian Jews prefer *zelebi*, a snail-shaped, deep-fried sweet. Israeli *sufganiyot*, which have replaced most of these sweets today as a celebratory treat, are basically raised jelly doughnuts and were probably adapted from the Greek *loukomades* and Austrian *pfannkuchen*.

Two Sisters, Two Cookbooks, Two Countries . . .

Elisabeth Rosenfeld

Growing up between the wars in the Hungarian village of Subotica (pronounced *Subotitsa*) near the then-Yugoslav border, the four Span sisters and their mother were known for their baking skills. Aranka, the eldest, born in 1899, even studied at the Cordon Bleu Cooking School in Paris. In the early 1930s, as a young mother with three children, Aranka wrote the first of her three cookbooks, *Zsidono Szakacskonyve* (Jewish Woman's Cookery Book), which became the bible of Jewish cookbooks for Hungarian women until World War II. Her second cookbook about inexpensive Jewish food was written in Hungarian in 1953 and published in Israel. It was she who taught her younger sister, Elisabeth, how to cook. Elisabeth would later bring her recipes across the ocean to Mexico City.

Born in 1905, Elisabeth Span married Ignatius Rosenfeld and moved to Belgrade, where he manufactured wood-burning stoves. The couple traveled a great deal throughout Europe and the Middle East to visit their clients. But in 1939, as war looked more and more certain, the Rosenfelds took an exploratory trip across the Atlantic to see where they might want to settle. They visited Toronto, the New York World's Fair, Bogotá, and Mexico City, to see Elisabeth's brother. "After that trip my mother claimed that the most beautiful cities in the world were Barcelona, Cairo, and Mexico City," said her son Peter Span, who now lives in Los Angeles. When the Rosenfelds returned home in September 1939, it was getting more difficult to leave. The Germans invaded Yugoslavia in 1941. As a Yugoslav reserve officer, Ignatius joined the army. He was eventually taken prisoner by the Germans and spent two years in a prisoner-of-war camp. Later, his wife, his three sons, and his wife's sisters' families were put in an Austrian forced-labor concentration camp, Ulrichkirchen, twenty miles from Vienna. Miraculously, the Rosenfeld family survived the war and were reunited briefly in April 1945, but Ignatius died several months later from sickness contracted in the camp.

Back home in Belgrade, Elisabeth and her sons had to share their home with two other families, the Communists considering their house too large for one. Elisabeth decided to emigrate, and in 1947, on a tourist visa, departed with her children for Mexico City, leaving behind everything she owned and her sister Aranka as well, who had lost much of her own family at Auschwitz. "She dared to leave her home and go with three small children across the world and make something out of them," said Jelena Blumenberg, Aranka's granddaughter, who came to the United States from Belgrade in 1972.

Like many other women in similar situations, Elisabeth began giving cooking lessons in her new home. "For lunch every day we ate the whole menu," recalled Peter, now fifty-eight. "My mother let the students taste the food, but she told them that this was her children's dinner. After school we helped deliver dobos tortes, strudels, and Prince Albert cakes to restaurants. It is still strange to me today that my mother was making the cakes for a restaurant called Pastelandia, 'Cake Land' in Spanish."

Elisabeth Rosenfeld was, in fact, the cooking teacher for a whole generation of upper-class Jewish and non-Jewish Mexican women. "It was an in thing to go there," said one of her former students. "She was a thin woman who spoke five languages, but none properly."

In the 1950s she opened Restaurant Elisabeth, which served Central European cooking and pastries. There she also gave lessons and wrote a cookbook, *Tres Cursos de Cocina Húngara y Yugoslava* (Three Courses of Hungarian and Yugoslav Cooking).

"Whenever I would walk into the kitchen to say hello to my mother, there would always be dough on the counter, a mixer always going and the kitchen smelling like warm chocolate, sugar, and eggs," said Peter. "I would dip my fingers into the chocolate cream from her Prince Albert Cake, I would take a handful of walnuts and nibble on them. This is how I remember my mother. She never talked about the Holocaust, but her cooking gave us a new life."

MEXICAN BANANA CAKE

FROM LISETTE SPAN

My friends are always asking me for a good banana cake recipe, and this is the best I have ever tasted. It comes from Lisette Span, the French-born daughter-in-law of Elisabeth Rosenfeld (see page 8), whom I met when I stayed at her pension in Zitacuaro, Mexico. This recipe came to Lisette from a visitor from the United States. She embellished it, and here it is. It has also traveled to Israel, where Elisabeth Rosenfeld's granddaughter is pastry chef at the Michael Andrew restaurant in Jerusalem.

2½ cups unbleached all-purpose flour
¾ cup plus 2 tablespoons sugar
1 teaspoon baking powder
1 teaspoon baking soda
½ teaspoon salt
½ cup vegetable oil
½ cup milk or water
3 large eggs, separated
1 teaspoon vanilla extract
4 large, ripe bananas, mashed (about 2 cups)
½ cup chopped walnuts (optional)
Confectioners' sugar (optional)

1. Preheat the oven to 350 degrees.
2. In a large mixing bowl, put the flour, ¾ cup of sugar, baking powder, baking soda, and salt. Add the oil, milk or water, egg yolks, vanilla, and mashed bananas and mix well. Stir in the walnuts.
3. Using an electric mixer, whip the egg whites until they form stiff peaks. Gently fold into the banana mixture.
4. Pour into a buttered and lightly floured 10-inch bundt pan or other tube pan and bake for 45–50 minutes, or until a toothpick inserted into the center comes out clean.

5. Allow the cake to cool for 10 minutes before removing it from the pan. Continue cooling it on a rack. When ready to serve it, sprinkle with the remaining 2 tablespoons sugar or with confectioners' sugar.

Yield: 8–10 servings (D or P)

CLASSIC RUGELACH

FROM ANN AMERNICK

Probably the most popular of American Jewish cookies, this horn-shaped treat was made in Europe with butter; cream cheese was added in this country. I *love* Ann's version: it has no sugar in the dough but a sprinkling on top of the finished cookie. She also uses this dough to make hamantashen.

The dough:
  8 ounces cream cheese, at room temperature
  1 cup (2 sticks) unsalted butter, at room temperature
  2 cups unbleached all-purpose flour
  Confectioners' sugar

Apricot filling:
  1 cup thick apricot preserves
  ¾ cup walnuts, roughly chopped

Chocolate filling:
  1 cup (about 8 ounces) shaved bittersweet chocolate, preferably
    imported
  ¼ cup sugar

Cinnamon-sugar filling:
  ¼ cup unsalted butter, melted
  ½ cup sugar
  2 teaspoons cinnamon

The dough:
1. Place the cream cheese and the butter in an electric mixer fitted with the paddle. Cream at a low speed until combined, about 2 minutes. Add the flour and mix until a very soft dough is formed, about 2 more minutes. Cover with plastic wrap and refrigerate for at least 2 hours.

Filling and baking the rugelach:

2. Preheat the oven to 350 degrees and line 2 cookie sheets with baking parchment.

3. Mix the ingredients for the apricot or chocolate filling and divide the dough into 4 balls. Roll the balls out into 4 circles about ⅛ inch thick and 9 inches in diameter. Spread the apricot or chocolate filling over the dough. If using the cinnamon-sugar filling, brush the melted butter on first, then the combined cinnamon and sugar.

4. Using a dull knife, cut each circle of dough into 16 pie-shaped pieces about 2 inches wide at the circumference. Roll up from the wide side to the center. Place the rugelach on the parchment-lined cookie sheets. Bake in the oven on the middle and lower racks, switching after 12 minutes, also switching back to front. Continue baking about 13 more minutes, or until golden brown. Remove the rugelach to racks to cool. Sprinkle the apricot and chocolate rugelach with confectioners' sugar just before serving.

Yield: 64 rugelach (D)

HUNGARIAN DOBOS TORTE

FROM ALEX LICHTMAN

When I was a child, I used to visit my grandparents in New York. My grandmother bought a dobos torte from Mrs. Herbst's Bakery for every birthday and holiday. To us children it was "seven-layer cake." In Hungarian, *dobos* means "like a drum," not just because the original was shaped like a little drum, but also because when you tap the caramel top crust of a true dobos torte, the caramel will resound like a drum. This cake takes care and time to prepare, but it is a wonderful challenge, well worth the effort.

Make sure you read the instructions through entirely before beginning this cake, and follow them exactly. It is very important to put the buttercream on the 6 layers, to refrigerate the layers, and then make the caramel for the seventh layer separately. Alex Lichtman used half butter and half vegetable shortening at Mrs. Herbst's, but in Hungary he would have used all butter. This delicious dobos torte is a tribute to Mrs. Herbst's Bakery, its bakers, and the magnificence of Austro-Hungarian pastries (see pages 88–89 for more on Alex Lichtman).

The cake:
   9 large egg whites
   1 cup sugar
   8 large egg yolks
   ¼ cup milk
   Grated peel of ½ lemon
   Pinch of salt
   1 teaspoon vanilla extract
   1½ cups unbleached all-purpose flour, sifted
   Softened unsalted butter for greasing the pans
   Flour for dusting

The chocolate buttercream filling:
   1½ cups (12 ounces) bittersweet chocolate, preferably imported, in
      pieces
   2 cups (4 sticks) plus 4 tablespoons unsalted butter, at room
      temperature
   Pinch of salt
   1 tablespoon vanilla extract
   4 cups confectioners' sugar, sifted
   2 large eggs

The caramel topping:
   ½ tablespoon cold vegetable shortening, for greasing the work surface
   1 cup sugar

The cake:
1. Preheat the oven to 400 degrees and cut two 10-inch circles out of card-
    board.
2. Beat the egg whites, gradually adding the sugar, until soft peaks are
    formed. Do not beat until stiff.
3. In an electric mixer fitted with the paddle, mix the egg yolks with the
    milk, lemon peel, salt, and vanilla, until well blended.
4. Gently fold the egg whites into the egg-yolk mixture; then fold in the
    flour until smooth.
5. Remove the sides from a 9-inch springform pan and grease it generously
    with softened butter. Dust with flour, then knock off the excess flour.
    Using a spatula, spread 1⅓ cups of the batter evenly over the pan bottom
    to a thickness of ⅛ inch, keeping an ⅛-inch border all around. Bake on the
    middle rack of the oven until brown spots appear on the layer, about 5–8
    minutes. Using a spatula, remove the cake layer from the pan, dust it
    lightly with flour right away, and put it on a cookie sheet to cool. Repeat 6
    more times, to make 7 layers.
6. Stack the cake layers with wax paper in between, cover them with a
    towel, and refrigerate several hours or overnight.

The chocolate buttercream filling:
7. Melt the chocolate in a double boiler over simmering water on low heat.
    Let it cool while you mix the buttercream.

8. For the buttercream, place the butter, salt, and vanilla in the bowl of an electric mixer fitted with the paddle. Beat on low speed for 3 minutes. Add the confectioners' sugar slowly and continue mixing on low speed for 2–3 more minutes.

9. Increase to medium speed for 4–5 minutes. Add the eggs, 1 at a time; then beat on high 4–5 minutes. Use a rubber scraper for the sides and the bottom of the mixing bowl.

10. Add the cooled, melted chocolate and mix for 3–4 minutes more at low speed.

Assembling six layers:

11. Place a cake layer on one of the cardboard circles and spread the top of it with buttercream to a ⅜-inch thickness all the way to the edge. Cover with another layer and press down lightly—this is important. Spread with another layer of buttercream, and repeat until 5 layers have been used. Top with a sixth layer, but do not cover with the buttercream; reserve the rest of the buttercream for the last layer and the sides of the cake. Smooth any buttercream that has been pressed out from between the layers around the sides of the cake. Place the cake in the refrigerator to set, about 5–6 hours. Refrigerate the remaining buttercream. Wrap the seventh layer with plastic and refrigerate.

The caramel topping:

12. Grease the surface of the second cardboard circle very lightly with vegetable shortening. Unwrap and place the seventh cake layer on top of the greased cardboard.

13. Pour the granulated sugar into an 8-inch non-stick skillet. Using a wooden spoon, stir the sugar over a high flame until it is halfway melted. Turn down the heat and keep stirring for about 3 minutes. Remove the pan from the heat and continue stirring until the sugar is a light caramel color and the thickness of heavy cream. Pour the caramel onto the middle of the seventh layer and spread swiftly, carefully, and evenly with an oiled knife (caramel hardens very fast). Spread it to the edges of this top layer. Quickly and lightly touch the dull edge of the oiled knife into the caramel on the cake to make 16 pie-shaped wedges, which are decorative and will be used as guidelines for cutting the cake. Oil the knife again

and retouch the markings. Remove this top layer from the cardboard and place it on a surface lightly dusted with granulated sugar so that it won't stick while the caramel cools.

Finishing the torte:

14. Remove the torte from the refrigerator, and smooth part of the remaining chocolate buttercream on top of the sixth cake layer. Lift the caramel-covered cake layer off the sugar onto the top of the torte. With a spatula, smooth the sides of the cake with the rest of the buttercream.
15. Refrigerate the torte until 15 minutes before serving.

Yield: one 9-inch round torte, cut in 16 slices (D)

CRANBERRY-WALNUT TART

FROM ANDRA TUNICK KARNOFSKY

Andra Tunick Karnofsky of Heavenly Hallah makes this cranberry-walnut tart at Chanukah because the red color of the cranberries reminds her of the flames of the menorah candles. It's a great winter dessert. At her family's Chanukah parties, her children Holden and Daliya and their friends work at cooking stations—one for *latke* frying, another for cookie cutting, and a third for filling Israeli *sufganiyot* (doughnuts) with jelly and sprinkling them with sugar (see *sufganiyot* recipe on pages 132–33).

The crust:
   1¾ cups unbleached all-purpose flour
   ¼ cup sugar
   ½ cup (1 stick) unsalted butter or parve margarine
   3 tablespoons vegetable shortening
   ¼ cup ice water

The filling:
   ⅔ cup light corn syrup
   ⅔ cup light-brown sugar
   3 large eggs
   1 teaspoon vanilla extract
   4 tablespoons unsalted butter or parve margarine, melted
   1½ cups coarsely chopped fresh cranberries
   1 cup coarsely chopped walnuts, toasted lightly (see Note on toasting
      nuts, page 69)

The crust:
1. Put the flour, sugar, butter or margarine, and vegetable shortening in a food processor fitted with the steel blade. Pulse until crumbly. Gradually add the ice water, processing until the dough forms a ball. Wrap the dough and refrigerate for at least 1 hour.

2. Preheat the oven to 350 degrees.
3. Remove the dough from the refrigerator and, on a floured surface, roll it into a circle 13 inches wide. Line a 10- or 11-inch tart pan with a removable bottom with the dough, trimming off the excess. Prick the dough with a fork.
4. Line the dough with baking parchment. Fill the baking parchment with dried beans, just enough to cover the paper. This helps set the crust by weighing down the dough as it bakes.
5. Bake for 10–12 minutes, or until the dough just begins to brown. Remove the beans and parchment and let the crust cool. Leave oven on at 350 degrees.

Filling and baking the tart:
6. Put the corn syrup and light-brown sugar in a mixing bowl and blend until smooth.
7. Beat in the eggs, 1 at a time, then the vanilla and the melted butter or margarine. Stir in the chopped cranberries and walnuts.
8. Pour the mixture into the partially baked and cooled pie crust.
9. Bake for 40–50 minutes, or until a knife inserted in the center of the pie comes out clean.

Yield: one 10- or 11-inch tart (D or P)

ISRAELI SUFGANIYOT
(Chanukah Jelly Doughnuts)

FROM BRIZEL'S BAKERY

The word *sufganiya*, a modern Hebrew word, comes from the Greek *sufgan*, meaning "puffed and fried." Every bakery in Jerusalem, no matter the ethnic origin of the baker, makes these jelly doughnuts for Chanukah. They used to consist of two rounds of dough sandwiching some jam, and the jam always ran out during the frying. Today, with new injectors on the market, balls of dough can be deep-fried first and then injected with jam before being rolled in sugar. This is a much easier, quicker way of doing them. And no jam escapes.

> 2 scant tablespoons (2 packages) active dry yeast
> 4 tablespoons sugar, plus sugar for rolling
> ¾ cup lukewarm water or milk
> 2½ cups unbleached all-purpose flour, sifted
> 2 large egg yolks
> Pinch of salt
> 1 teaspoon ground cinnamon
> 1½ tablespoons unsalted butter or parve margarine, at room
>   temperature
> Vegetable oil for deep-frying
> ½ cup plum, strawberry, or apricot jam

1. Sprinkle the yeast and 2 tablespoons of the sugar into the water or milk and stir to dissolve.
2. Place the flour on a work surface and make a well in the center. Add the yeast mixture, egg yolks, salt, cinnamon, and the remaining 2 tablespoons sugar. Knead well, about 5 minutes, working the butter or margarine into the dough and kneading until the dough is elastic. You can also use a food processor fitted with the steel blade to do this, processing about 2 minutes.

3. Put the dough in a greased bowl, cover with plastic, and let it rise overnight in the refrigerator.
4. Sprinkle flour on the work surface. Roll out the dough to an ⅛-inch thickness. Using a 2-inch cookie cutter or floured drinking glass, cut out circles. Let the dough circles rise 15 minutes more.
5. With your hands, gently form the dough circles into balls.
6. Pour 2 inches of oil into a heavy pot and heat until very hot, about 375 degrees.
7. Slip the doughnuts into the oil, 4 or 5 at a time, using a slotted spoon. Turn them when brown, after a few minutes, to crisp on the other side. Drain on paper towels.
8. Using a turkey baster or an injector available at cooking stores, inject a teaspoon of jam into each doughnut. Then roll all of them in granulated sugar and serve immediately. You can make larger *sufganiyot* if you like.

Yield: twenty-four 2-inch-wide **sufganiyot** *(D or P)*

PURIM

YEAST-DOUGH HAMANTASHEN,
from Alex Lichtman

HEAVENLY HAMANTASHEN,
from Andra Tunick Karnofsky

NANA'S PRUNE AND NUT ROLL,
from Michael London

TRAVADOS,
from Zohar Cohen-Nehemia Halleen

ERASS B'ADJWAH,
from Mansoura Middle Eastern Pastries

*Therefore do the Jews of the villages, that dwell in the unwalled towns, make
the fourteenth day of the month of Adar a day of gladness and feasting,
and a good day, and of sending portions to one another.*

MEGILLAT ESTHER 9:19

Purim places a greater emphasis on festivity and delights than does any
other Jewish holiday. Celebrated on the 14th day of Adar, which falls
in late February or early March, the day is a reminder of the Jews'
deliverance from the threat of destruction in ancient times. The wicked
Haman, chief minister of the Persian King Ahasuerus, wished to exterminate
all the Jews of the Persian empire because he thought the Jew Mordechai had
failed to show him proper respect. But King Ahasuerus's queen, the beautiful Esther, was also (unbeknownst to him) a Jew, the niece and ward of
Mordechai. At the risk of her own life, she helped Mordechai foil Haman's
wicked plot. On the 13th of Adar, the Jews were to be destroyed. Instead, the
evil decree was revoked, and it was the Jews who triumphed over their
would-be persecutors. The victory that they celebrated is recalled every year
in the festival of Purim.

The festival is celebrated by two recountings of the story of the *Megillah*
(the Book of Esther) in the synagogue (on the eve and the day of Purim); a
seudat Purim, or festival meal, in the late afternoon of Purim; charity to the
poor—usually in the form of money to at least two people; and the sending
of gifts to friends and neighbors (*mishloach manot*). Prior to the festival, a day
of fasting—the *Taanit Esther*—recalls the three-day fast Esther made before
undertaking the dangerous task of approaching the king uninvited to plead
for her people. Gifts, charity, and fasting are all required for repentance, and
it is because of repentance, we are told, that the Jews were saved.

In the seasonal cycle of Jewish holidays, Purim's gastronomic position is
quite important. As the last festival prior to Passover, it is an occasion to
splurge with risen flour, so many delicacies, deep-fried and baked, are prepared for this holiday. In Eastern Europe before World War II, for example,
women baked strudels, *taiglach* (see pages 68–69), *kichel* (see pages 50–51),
and of course, hamantashen. In Morocco, women bake small breads filled
with hard-boiled eggs. In Iraq and Syria, they make all kinds of *sambusak,* or

turnovers filled with chicken or cheese (pages 183–84). In Tunisia, Lebanon, and Egypt, deep-fried pastries filled with nuts and oozing with honey are prepared.

The many varieties of baked goods are prepared as the gifts offered at Purim. At least two different kinds of food are placed on a tray. One should be of flour, like hamantashen or a piece of honey cake, and one of a fruit, like dried figs or an orange. My mother-in-law remembers how special it was in Poland to receive an orange from Palestine at Purim. In my family, we try to send *mishloach manot* to neighbors and elderly friends who are often forgotten.

On Hamantashen

As in so many questions Jewish, there are disputes as to the origin of the word *hamantash* in Yiddish. Some say it comes from *Hamin tash kocho,* meaning, "May Haman's strength become weak." Others say it was merely Haman's three-cornered hat. And then there is the theory that *mun-tasche* (bag of poppy seeds) is the correct name, *hamantash* being merely a corruption of it. A *midrash* (a traditional allegory) states that the three corners of the cookie represent the three Patriarchs, Abraham, Isaac, and Jacob.

The filling is as symbolic as the dough. Since Purim is the one time of year Jews were permitted to drink and eat to excess, it made sense to have a pastry filled with poppy seeds, a part of the flower renowned for its powerful drug. Like kreplach, a filled dumpling also eaten at Purim, hamantashen are covered foods, their essence hidden within.

YEAST-DOUGH HAMANTASHEN

FROM ALEX LICHTMAN

Hamantashen are traditional at Purim, and there are myriad variations on Haman in cookie form—for instance, Egyptians eat *oznei Haman,* a deep-fried sweet shaped like Haman's ears, and Hungarian and German Jews eat *kindli* or *beigli,* filled cookies. Alex Lichtman, of Mrs. Herbst's Bakery, probably transformed the *kindli* or *beigli* into a yeast hamantashen dough as opposed to using a cookie dough, more common in the United States. Whenever I make a speech about Jewish food, there is invariably someone asking for a hamantashen yeast dough. Here it is.

    3 scant tablespoons (3 envelopes) active dry yeast
    4½ tablespoons warm milk
    1 cup plus ½ teaspoon sugar
    2 cups (4 sticks) unsalted butter, cold
    ¾ teaspoon salt
    1 teaspoon vanilla extract
    1 teaspoon grated lemon peel
    7 cups unbleached all-purpose flour, plus ½ cup for dusting
    1 cup sour cream
    3 large eggs
    Filling of choice (see below)

The dough:
1. In a small bowl, dissolve the yeast in the milk, sprinkled with ½ teaspoon of the sugar.
2. In an electric mixer fitted with the paddle, combine the butter, salt, vanilla, lemon peel, and remaining sugar. Beat at low speed for 3 minutes.
3. Add 7 cups of the flour. Beat at low speed for 4 minutes more.
4. Add the sour cream, 2 of the eggs, and the yeast mixture. Beat at medium

speed for 4–5 minutes, until the dough separates easily from the sides of the bowl.

5. Divide the dough into 4 pieces, and then each piece into 9. You will have 36 equal pieces. Shape them into balls and put them in a large bowl. Cover and refrigerate for 15 minutes.

6. Dust a work surface very lightly with some of the remaining ½ cup flour. Roll the balls out into ovals about 2¼ inches long by 2 inches wide (or, if you want larger ones, 3 inches long by 2½ inches wide).

Assembling and baking the hamantashen:

7. Place 1 heaping teaspoon of the filling in the center of each oval. Make 12 at a time, setting them side by side. To make the three-cornered-hat shape, lift the 2 longer sides of the oval over the filling, making a point at the top. Then fold the remaining short edge up to meet the folded long sides, making a triangle. Gently shape the 3 closed edges and smooth out the surface. There should be no filling visible.

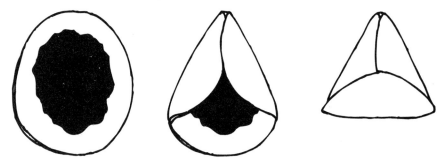

8. In a small bowl, beat the remaining egg.

9. Lightly grease 2 large cookie sheets. Place the hamantashen on the sheets 1½ inches apart.

10. Lightly brush the tops of the hamantashen with the beaten egg and allow to dry. Let them rise for 30–35 minutes and brush again with the beaten egg. At the center of each top, put a pinch of plain ground walnuts for the hamantashen filled with nut filling and a pinch of plain poppy seeds for those with the poppy-seed filling. Allow to dry for 20–25 more minutes. Meanwhile, preheat the oven to 375 degrees.

11. Bake the hamantashen on the middle rack for 16–20 minutes, or until golden.

Yield: 36 hamantashen (D)

Poppy-Seed Filling

This filling is best made 1–2 days before use.

⅔ cup water
¼ teaspoon cinnamon
¾ cup sugar
¼ cup raisins
2½–3 teaspoons grated orange peel
½ teaspoon grated lemon peel
2 tablespoons honey
2 cups poppy seeds*
3 tablespoons cake crumbs (from pound cake or other leftover cake)

1. Bring the water to a boil in a medium saucepan. Whisk in the cinnamon.
2. Add the sugar, raisins, orange peel, lemon peel, and honey, and return to a boil.
3. Lower the heat, add the poppy seeds and the cake crumbs, and stir well with a wooden spoon. Simmer on low heat for 5–6 minutes.
4. Pour into a bowl, cover tightly with plastic wrap, and refrigerate. It will keep for up to 2 weeks.

Yield: 2¼ cups, fills about 36 hamantashen (P)

Nut Filling

This filling is best made 1–2 days before use.

½ cup plus 1 tablespoon cold water
¼ teaspoon cinnamon

---

* Available at health food stores, where they are sold in bulk and are much cheaper than the commercial varieties sold elsewhere.

¾ cup sugar
2 tablespoons raisins
1½ tablespoons grated orange peel
½ teaspoon grated lemon peel
2 tablespoons honey
2¼ cups coarsely ground pecans or walnuts
2 tablespoons cake crumbs (from pound cake or other leftover cake)

1. Bring the water to a boil in a medium saucepan. Whisk in the cinnamon.
2. Add the sugar, raisins, orange peel, lemon peel, and honey, and return to a boil.
3. Add the nuts and the cake crumbs and stir well with a wooden spoon. Simmer on low heat for 3–4 minutes.
4. Pour into a bowl, cover tightly with plastic wrap, and refrigerate. It will keep for up to 2 weeks.

Yield: 2¼ cups, fills about 36 hamantashen (P)

HEAVENLY HAMANTASHEN

FROM ANDRA TUNICK KARNOFSKY

At Purim, Andra of Heavenly Hallah makes a meal with all foods shaped like triangles—potatoes, carrots, spinach phyllo, gefilte-fish patties, even peanut butter–chocolate mousse, and, of course, hamantashen stuffed with apricot, strawberry, or prune lekvar or jam, or chocolate chips. If you can find lekvar, often made from dried apricots or prunes, use that rather than regular fruit preserves because it holds together much better in baking. You can always use the poppy-seed or nut fillings on pages 141–42. This dough is the more common cookie dough used in the United States.

½ cup (1 stick) unsalted butter or parve margarine, at room temperature
1 cup sugar
1 large egg, beaten
2 tablespoons orange juice
½ teaspoon vanilla extract
2 teaspoons baking powder
½ teaspoon salt
2 tablespoons wheat germ
2 cups unbleached all-purpose flour
Filling of choice

1. In a food processor fitted with the steel blade, cream together the butter or margarine and sugar. Pulse just a few seconds. Or use your fingers or 2 forks to crumble the butter together with the sugar in a large mixing bowl.
2. Add the beaten egg, orange juice, vanilla, baking powder, and salt and mix well, again just a few seconds in the processor. Add the wheat germ and the flour, ½ cup at a time. If you use a food processor, the mixture will come together in a ball. Or you may use your fingers to mix the

ingredients and shape the dough into a ball. Wrap and refrigerate the dough for 2 hours.

3. Preheat the oven to 375 degrees and grease 2 cookie sheets.
4. On a lightly floured work surface, roll out the dough to an ⅛-inch thickness. Cut in circles with a 2-inch cookie cutter or the floured rim of a 2-inch glass. Place 1 tablespoon of the filling of your choice in the center of the circle. Pinch together 3 corners evenly spaced along the edge of the circle to form a triangular hamantashen shape. Some of the filling will show in the center. Arrange the cookies on the cookie sheets 1 inch apart.
5. Bake 1 sheet at a time on the middle rack of the oven for 10–12 minutes, until the hamantashen are light golden brown.

Yield: 48 hamantashen (D or P)

NOTE: Possible fillings for hamantashen include nuts, poppy seeds, apricot, strawberry, or prune lekvar or jam, lemon curd, and chocolate chips.

NANA'S PRUNE AND NUT ROLL

FROM MICHAEL LONDON

Michael London's grandmother's cookie roll, similar to my great-aunt's cookies (see *The Jewish Holiday Kitchen,* page 169), is a perfect alternative to prune hamantashen at Purim and a delicious dessert any time of year. His grandmother Betty Seltzer, known to Michael as Nana Banana or Betty Baby, was famous in Brooklyn for her gefilte fish and her baked goods. Born in New York, she learned this recipe from her mother, who came from Austria-Hungary. Although Michael remembers his grandmother making the lekvar from prunes, his great-grandmother probably dried freestone plums herself and then made the jam. You can substitute prepared apricot or prune levkar or good preserves, allowing 1 cup per roll.

The crust:
  1 cup (2 sticks) unsalted butter or parve margarine,* at room
      temperature
  1 cup sugar
  ¼ teaspoon salt
  3–3½ cups unbleached all-purpose flour
  2½ teaspoons baking powder
  3 large eggs
  1 teaspoon vanilla extract
  Grated peel and juice of 1 orange

The filling:
  3 cups pitted prunes
  2 cups water
  ½ teaspoon cinnamon
  1 tablespoon sugar
  1 cup chopped walnuts

* Although I have included parve margarine, the Londons would never use a substitute for butter.

The crust:

1. Blend the butter, sugar, and salt in the bowl of an electric mixer fitted with the dough hook or a food processor fitted with the steel blade.
2. In a separate bowl, mix together 3 cups of the flour and the baking powder.
3. Add 2 of the eggs, the vanilla, orange peel, and orange juice to the sugar-butter mixture. Blend for a few minutes or process a few seconds. Then add the flour mixture and mix again just until incorporated. Depending on the juiciness of the orange, you may have to add more flour.
4. Divide the dough into 3 pieces and pat into 3 rectangles about 3½ by 6 inches. Cover each with plastic wrap and refrigerate a few hours or overnight.

Filling and baking the rolls:

5. Put the prunes and water in a saucepan and simmer, uncovered, for 45 minutes, or until the prunes are soft enough to break apart with the back of a fork and most of the water has evaporated. Be sure to watch the prunes so that they don't burn. Add more water if needed. Once the prunes are done, remove them from the pan and mash them.
6. Preheat the oven to 325 degrees and mix the cinnamon and sugar in a small bowl. Cover a cookie sheet with baking parchment.
7. Dust a work surface with flour and roll out 1 rectangle of the dough, turning and flipping it occasionally, until it measures about 8 by 11 inches. Sprinkle it with a little cinnamon-sugar.
8. Using a plastic spatula, spread one third of the prune filling lengthwise along one side in a 4-inch-wide strip, leaving a 1-inch border. Then sprinkle one third of the walnuts over the prunes. You should still have a 3-inch-wide strip of bare dough.
9. Beat the remaining egg and brush it in another 2-inch stripe on the bare part of the dough, alongside the filling, leaving 1 inch bare at the edge.
10. Starting from the long edge with the fillings, roll up the dough like a jelly roll. Pinch the ends under and place this roll seam side down on the parchment-lined cookie sheet. Sprinkle with more cinnamon-sugar. Repeat the process with the other 2 pieces of dough.
11. Bake the rolls on the middle oven rack for 45–60 minutes, or until lightly browned. Cut with a sharp knife into ½-inch slices

Yield: 3 rolls or 45 cookies (D or P)

TRAVADOS (Jerusalem Cinnamon-Nut Cookies)

FROM ZOHAR COHEN-NEHEMIA HALLEEN

Zohar remembers these sweet walnut-stuffed cookies as *burekas,* called that because of their crescent shape. They are an old Jerusalem Sephardic treat, similar to *mahmoul,* a nut-filled cookie often pressed into a wooden mold that prints a design on top. *Travados* are traditionally served on all holidays, but particularly at Purim. They taste even better the second day.

1¼ cups (2½ sticks) unsalted butter or parve margarine, at room
    temperature
1¼ cups plus 2 tablespoons sugar
1 teaspoon vanilla extract
Dash of salt
4 cups unbleached all-purpose flour
2 cups plus 1 teaspoon ice water
1½ cups walnuts
¾ teaspoon cinnamon
1 large egg yolk
Juice of ½ lemon

1. Place the butter or margarine and 2 tablespoons of the sugar in a food processor fitted with the steel blade and process a few seconds. Add the vanilla, salt, and flour. Pulse to combine, then gradually add ½ cup of the water as you pulse until a soft dough is formed. Set aside.
2. Using a food processor fitted with the steel blade, grind 1 cup of the walnuts with the cinnamon and ¼ cup of the sugar. Then add the remaining ½ cup of nuts and roughly chop.
3. Divide the dough into 4 pieces. On a work surface lightly dusted with flour, roll each piece of dough out into a circle ⅛ inch thick. Using a 3-inch round cookie cutter or floured rim of a glass, cut out circles. Place 1 heaping teaspoon of the walnut mixture in the center of each circle. Fold

over, crimp the edges to seal, and shape into a crescent. Repeat until the dough is used up.

4. Beat the egg yolk and the teaspoon of ice water and brush onto the cookies.

5. Preheat the oven to 350 degrees and grease 2 cookie sheets.

6. Place the cookies about 1 inch apart on the sheets, and bake 1 sheet at a time on the bottom rack of the oven for 15–20 minutes. Cool the *travados* on a rack.

7. While the *travados* are baking, bring the remaining 1 cup sugar and the remaining 1½ cups water to a boil and simmer about 15 minutes. Add the lemon juice and return to a boil. Remove from the heat.

8. Using a slotted spoon, submerge the hot cookies in the warm syrup. Remove the cookies and place on a cooling rack. Alternatively, you can simply roll the cookies in confectioners' sugar.

Yield: 48 **travados** *(D or P)*

ERASS B'ADJWAH (Syrian Date-filled Crescents)

FROM MANSOURA MIDDLE EASTERN PASTRIES

For Syrian Jews, dates are not only a sign of welcome throughout the year but also a symbol of sweetness for the new year. "In the Syrian community, we eat *adjwah* at every holiday except for Passover," said Josiane Mansoura. The Mansouras pat out the dough with the palms of their hands while other bakers such as Sarina Roffe, also from this community, use a tortilla press to flatten the dough. Although the Mansouras make their *adjwah* without walnuts, I've included them as an option.

The dough:
    1 cup *smead* (semolina, not semolina flour)*
    2 cups unbleached all-purpose flour
    Dash of salt
    1 tablespoon vegetable oil
    1 cup (2 sticks) unsalted butter or parve margarine, at room
        temperature
    ½–¾ cup cold water

The filling:
    1 pound pitted dates
    1–2 cups water
    ½ cup chopped walnuts (optional)
    2 tablespoons grated orange peel
    ½ cup confectioners' sugar

1. Place the semolina, flour, salt, oil, and butter or margarine in a food processor fitted with the steel blade. Process, adding the water a little at a time, until the dough forms a ball. You can also make it by hand as the

* Available at Middle Eastern markets.

older Syrians do: Pour the semolina, flour, and salt in a bowl. With a fork or your fingers, mix in the oil and butter until the dough is lumpy. Do not overmix. Add the water, a little at a time, until the dough comes together and is smooth and pliable.

2. Remove the dough from the food processor, cover, and let it rest. At this point you can refrigerate the dough to continue at a later time, bringing it to room temperature before working it.

3. Grind the dates in the food processor fitted with the steel blade. Then scoop into a saucepan, add water barely to cover, and cook the dates over low heat, stirring occasionally, for about 15 minutes, or until the water is mostly absorbed and a thick date paste is formed. Stir in the nuts and orange peel. Let the filling cool.

4. Preheat the oven to 350 degrees.

5. Separate the dough into 4 equal parts and divide each part into nine 2-inch balls. Flatten each with a rolling pin, the palm of your hand, or a tortilla press to a 4-inch diameter. If using a tortilla press, flour it or cover

it with plastic wrap so the dough doesn't stick to the press. Place 1 tablespoon of the date mixture in the middle of the circle of dough, pressing
the dates down on the circle. Fold into a half-moon shape to enclose, gently pinch the edges along the round side to seal in the date mixture, and
then shape into a crescent. Repeat with the remaining dough and filling.
You may have about 3 tablespoons of filling left; this makes a great
hamantashen filling.

6. Bake on the middle rack of the oven on an ungreased cookie sheet for
   20–25 minutes, or until slightly golden. The *adjwah* can be frozen after
   they cool. Sprinkle with confectioners' sugar when ready to serve.

Yield: 36 adjwah *(D or P)*

PASSOVER

ITALIAN MATZAH,
from Edda Servi Machlin

BISCOTTI DI PESACH DELLA MAMMA,
from Edda Servi Machlin

MACARONES,
from Elisabeth Rosenfeld

PRINCE ALBERT CAKE,
from Elisabeth Rosenfeld

PASSOVER CHOCOLATE CAKE,
from Ann Amernick

**MERINGUE BASKETS
WITH LIME CREAM JEAN-LOUIS,**
from Ann Amernick

PASSOVER SPONGE CAKE,
from Helen Silverberg

For seven days, matzot you are to eat, already on the first day
you are to get rid of leaven from your houses, for anyone who eats
what is fermented—from the first day to the seventh
day—: that person shall be cut off from Israel!

EXODUS 12:15

Passover is one of the world's oldest continually observed festivals, and despite intrusions of modernity, it retains its ancient charm. During this celebration of the commemoration of the Exodus from Egypt, Jews do not eat leavened or fermented food for eight days (even in Israel). A reading of the Haggadah—a narration of the Exodus—is a central part of the first (and second) night of Passover.

Following the biblical injunction, houses are thoroughly cleaned to remove anything that has a trace of leavening, including regular flour. To compensate for the absence of flour demanded by this ancient rule, Jews the world over have created all kinds of baked goods from soaked matzah and, later, matzah cake meal (almost the consistency of regular flour but without the name). Flourless tortes using ground nuts, sponge cakes made from matzah meal or potato flour, macaroons, *krimsel,* and other Passover fritters are all favorites during this eight-day holiday.

The Bread of Affliction and Freedom

The eating and baking of matzah, besides being central to the history of Jewish food, have always reflected the times and spirit of the Jews themselves. In Exodus, unleavened bread symbolizes both affliction and the journey to freedom. It is what the Hebrews ate, with the bitter herbs, as they fled Egypt (Exodus 12:31–39); it was made part of their ensuing celebrations of Passover (Exodus 12:15–20); and it became a sacrament in their priestly rituals (Exodus 29:2).

The earliest matzah was probably made of barley, the word *matzah* coming from the Old Babylonian *maassaartum,* which means "barley." It was the first grain harvested in the Middle East, used for many centuries before wheat appeared, about 4000 B.C.E. Later, however, only wheat came to be used, a practice that continues today.

Each year in the spring, long before the Exodus, the Hebrews celebrated a Festival of Unleavened Bread in thanks for the new grains after the barley planting. When they went to Egypt they learned about yeast, and in their flight from Egypt the original spring festival became a patriotic one devoted to freedom. Matzah represents the Jews' flight from Egypt, when they had no time to let their bread rise, or bake properly. In Exodus, God describes this feast: "They are to eat the flesh on that night, roasted in fire, and matzot, with bitter herbs they are to eat it" (Exodus 12:8). At the Passover seder, Jews recited their traditional Sabbath blessing over three matzot, which eventually came to symbolize the three classes of Jews—Cohen, Levi, and Israel. At the seder the first food eaten is parsley or potatoes, followed by a piece of matzah. Later, one eats a symbolic "sandwich" of matzah and bitter herbs, which have been dipped in the *haroset,* a paste of nuts and fruits symbolic of the mortar made by the Israelite slaves in Egypt.

Until the advent of machine-made matzah at the end of the nineteenth century, Jews made their own, or bought it directly from their synagogues, where special committees shaped matzah by hand into round or rectangular forms. "When I lived in Germany," said Paula Stern Kissinger, ninety-six, "we bought matzah flour from our shul and brought it to a communal oven to be baked. Together we baked enough matzah for our entire family."

In addition to manufacturing matzah, companies like Manischewitz made matzah meal from broken pieces and packaged it so cooks could make dishes such as "airy matzah balls." They also packaged matzah meal. For centuries before this, leftover matzah had been made into crumbs with a large wooden mortar and pestle. Early American immigrant recipes, for example, call for broken-up matzah to be made into matzah balls or *krimsel.*

Purists today use handmade, or *shmurah,* matzah. Prepared in bakeries like D. and T. Matzah Bakery in Crown Heights, Brooklyn, this matzah is served to a dedicated and ever-increasing clientele. D. and T. produces about 12,000–15,000 pounds of *shmurah* matzah each year. "*Shmurah* matzah means it is watched or supervised from when the wheat is cut until after it is baked," says Isaac Tenenbaum, the owner. The wheat comes from small farms in New Jersey, Pennsylvania, and upstate New York and is ground in local mills kashered for Passover runs.

In this tiny bakery, with walls and tables protected with brown paper, the carefully watched flour is mixed with pure spring water from wells in Brooklyn, rolled with a long, narrow wooden rolling pin, pricked (to reduce air bubbles, which may enhance the forbidden fermentation), baked, and stacked, all within the stipulated eighteen minutes. The men and women working do it very quickly, yelling, "Matzah, matzah!" when their rolled-out dough is ready for the oven. "The law is that only eighteen minutes can elapse from when the water touches the flour until when it goes in the oven," said Rabbi Tenenbaum. After eighteen minutes it expands, and is no longer kosher for Passover.

As Reuven Sirota shovels the hand-formed matzah into the brick oven, he recalls his native Uzbekistan, which he left in the 1970s. "Making matzah is a *mitzvah*," he says. "In Uzbekistan, I had to make it in secret at four o'clock in the morning. It was forbidden for Jews to celebrate Passover. For me, making matzah openly represents the freedom of living in America."

❖   ❖   ❖

Edda Servi Machlin, author of *The Classic Cuisine of the Italian Jews,* also felt this *mitzvah* (see page 67 for her story of World War II). "While we were hiding in Italy, every night as Easter approached during that spring of '44, we carefully watched the moon. We knew that when it would be as round as a wheel of cheese, it would be the fourteenth of Nissan, the first night of Passover. We began to make a few matzot with the flour that the farmer who was sheltering us allotted to us, and baked them in the rustic stone oven that was built outside. The farmers had never seen unleavened bread before and gathered around to watch us make these round and oval cakes, about a quarter inch thick and cut and trimmed like doilies. But for us, not only did they symbolize the festival of remembrance and freedom, they also represented home. By being able to make and bake our own matzah, something we used to do with our parents as little children, we nourished our souls even more than our stomachs."

In the Middle Ages, matzah often had decorations on it, and in some countries, such as Italy, it was almost an inch thick and did not crumble. This thick *afikomen,* the hidden or "dessert" matzah, became a symbol of good luck. Jews of medieval Italy used matzah as an amulet, hanging it in the house throughout the year or carrying it in a pouch or wallet, a practice continued by some Italian Jews even now.

Today Edda, in her home outside New York City, still makes the elaborate matzah of her childhood, in honor of the past. "The trick," she said, "is to use flour with absolutely no bran in it, so that no fermentation takes place."

ITALIAN MATZAH (Azzima Semplice Pitiglianese)

FROM EDDA SERVI MACHLIN

Try this recipe with children. The decorative matzah will be a hands-on introduction to the traditions of the Italian Jews. Of course, to be truly correct for Passover, matzah making must be rabbinically supervised.

3½ cups cold spring water
7 cups matzah cake meal

1. Preheat the oven to 550 degrees.
2. In a large bowl, quickly mix the water with enough of the matzah cake meal to form a very stiff dough. Spread the remaining cake meal on a smooth working surface (preferably marble or glass) and turn the dough out over it. Knead with force for 3 minutes. During the first phase of kneading, make a few cuts in the dough with a sharp knife, which will enable you to incorporate more cake meal into it. Continue to knead quickly until the dough is perfectly smooth.
3. Divide the dough into 12 equal parts (at this point, the more people helping, the better). Have each of your helpers knead the little pieces of dough until elastic. With rolling pins, roll into 9- by 5-inch ovals or into circles 6½ inches in diameter.
4. To finish the edges and make rings of holes, place your thumb at an angle to the edge of the circle of dough and then pinch with your thumb and index finger to create a small bump. Repeat this motion at the same angle all around so that the bumps are the same distance apart. Now for the holes: A quarter inch from the pinched border, pinch a piece of dough with your thumb and index finger, creating 1 small tear on each side of the

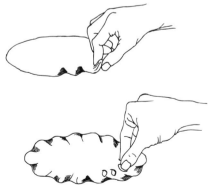

pinch. Move the thumb into the hole made by the index finger and pinch the dough again with the 2 fingers, following the shape of the dough and repeating the process above. Continue all around until an outer ring of holes is completed. About a quarter inch in from the outer ring, pinch the dough and make another ring of holes to make a decorative circle. Repeat until you have 3 concentric rings of holes. At this point, your matzah will look like a doily and be almost ready to bake. Repeat this process with all the circles of dough.

5. Place the matzot on an ungreased cookie sheet. With a metal comb or fork, prick tiny holes all over the matzot to prevent swelling and blistering during baking.
6. Bake in the oven on the middle rack for 6–7 minutes, or until the matzot are pale brown.

Yield: 12 matzot (P)

BISCOTTI DI PESACH DELLA MAMMA
(Mother's Passover Biscotti)

FROM EDDA SERVI MACHLIN

"Mandelbrot is almost the same thing as biscotti," said Edda Servi Machlin. "We made them for Pesach with no leavening." According to Edda, the word *biscotti* in Italy has come to designate all sorts of hard cookies, but in the United States it has retained the original meaning—*bis* derives from Latin and means "once more, twice," and *cotti* is Italian for "cooked." Biscotti are just that—cooked twice; so are mandelbrot (in Yiddish), which comes from *mandel* (almond) and *brot* (bread). Which came first? Ah, there is the question, but certainly they are linked. This particular recipe came from Edda's mother, Sara Di Capua, who was born in Rome. Serve them à la Machlin, with sweet vermouth and tea. During the year, substitute all-purpose flour for the matzah cake meal.

1⅓ cups sugar
½ teaspoon salt
⅓ cup olive oil
1 teaspoon vanilla extract
1 teaspoon almond extract
3 large eggs
3 cups matzah cake meal
1 cup whole almonds

1. In an electric mixer fitted with the paddle or by hand, cream together the sugar, salt, oil, vanilla, and almond extract. Add the eggs, 1 at a time, beating after each addition.
2. Add enough matzah cake meal to make a soft but manageable dough. Fold in the whole almonds.
3. Preheat the oven to 350 degrees and grease a cookie sheet.
4. Spoon the dough onto an oiled work surface and divide into 3 parts. Oil

your hands and shape the dough into 3 cylinders, each 15 inches long. Place on the cookie sheet and bake on the middle rack for 25 minutes.

5. Remove from the oven. Raise the temperature to 450 degrees. Slice through each cylinder diagonally, making approximately 20 slices per cylinder. Lay the slices flat on a greased baking sheet and bake on the middle rack of the oven for 10 more minutes.

6. Cool the biscotti thoroughly before storing.

Yield: about 60 biscotti (P)

MACARONES (Passover Macaroons)

FROM ELISABETH ROSENFELD

These macaroons, made from almonds or hazelnuts and egg whites, are very elegant. I recommend using baking parchment when making them.

2 cups blanched almonds or peeled hazelnuts, plus 15 whole blanched almonds or peeled hazelnuts for garnish
1 cup sugar
3 large egg whites, unbeaten
½ tablespoon lemon juice
Dash of salt

1. In a food processor fitted with the steel blade, grind the 2 cups of almonds or peeled hazelnuts with the sugar until the nuts are finely chopped but not pulverized. You could also use a metate, or grinding stone, as Elisabeth Rosenfeld did in Mexico. Put the ground nuts in a bowl.
2. Stir in the unbeaten egg whites, lemon juice, and salt.
3. Preheat the oven to 350 degrees and line a cookie sheet with baking parchment.
4. Roll a heaping teaspoon of dough between your palms to make a ball. Place on the cookie sheet, and compress it slightly. Insert half a blanched almond or hazelnut into the top. Repeat with the rest of the dough, leaving 4 inches between each cookie.
5. Bake on the middle oven rack for 18–20 minutes, or until the cookies spread and brown a little. Remove them from the oven, cool, and separate with a spatula, taking care not to break them.

Yield: about 30 large macaroons (P)

NOTE: A half teaspoon of almond extract may be used instead of lemon juice.

PRINCE ALBERT CAKE

FROM ELISABETH ROSENFELD

Of all Elisabeth Rosenfeld's desserts, the most popular with her children was the Prince Albert cake, named for Queen Victoria's handsome German husband. "It was chocolate over chocolate," recalled Elisabeth's son Peter, now in his fifties, "She used Mexican chocolate and Dutch Dröste cocoa. We ate this cake at Passover and on other special occasions." Now my family eats it at Passover and for birthdays during the year, when I substitute regular flour for the matzah cake meal.

> 1½ cups (3 sticks) plus 2 tablespoons unsalted butter or parve margarine, at room temperature
> 2 cups sugar
> 10 large eggs, separated
> 9 ounces bittersweet chocolate, broken into pieces
> 1 tablespoon matzah cake meal
> 3 ounces bittersweet chocolate for grating

1. In an electric mixer fitted with the paddle or by hand in a large bowl, cream the butter with half the sugar, adding the egg yolks 1 at a time to the mixture and beating a few seconds after each addition.
2. In a separate bowl, beat the egg whites until stiff, while gradually adding the remaining 1 cup sugar.
3. Melt the 9 ounces of bittersweet chocolate in the top of a double boiler over simmering water. Cool and slowly beat the chocolate into the egg-yolk mixture. Gently fold in the egg whites.
4. Preheat the oven to 350 degrees and oil a 12- by 18-inch baking pan; line it with baking parchment that has been oiled and sprinkled with the matzah cake meal. Spread two thirds of the cake batter evenly in the pan and bake on the middle rack for 30 minutes.
5. Cover the remaining batter and refrigerate.

6. Remove the cake from the pan and let it cool completely. Cut horizontally, into two layers, and spread the top of the bottom layer with half the refrigerated batter. Cover the batter layer with the top layer of the cake; then spread on the rest of the batter. Garnish with the grated chocolate. Refrigerate until ready to serve. When cutting, use a knife dipped into hot water, and cut into 3-inch squares.

Yield: 24 squares (D or P)

PASSOVER CHOCOLATE CAKE

FROM ANN AMERNICK

"I created this cake because people are always asking me for a good choco-late Passover dessert," said pastry chef Ann Amernick. "Most recipes call for cocoa and potato starch. Here I use real chocolate, which gives the cake a wonderfully dense texture. The key is to use imported bittersweet chocolate, the only true chocolate, and not to mask it with too much sugar."

10 ounces good imported bittersweet chocolate, broken into pieces
½ cup (1 stick) unsalted butter or parve margarine,* at room
    temperature
½ cup sugar, plus more for sprinkling
5 large eggs, separated
⅓ cup finely ground almonds (done in a food processor)
2 tablespoons kosher-for-Passover brandy
Whipped cream (optional)
Fresh raspberries (optional)

1. Preheat the oven to 300 degrees and grease well a 9-inch springform pan; line the bottom with baking parchment.
2. Melt the chocolate in a double boiler over barely simmering water. When the chocolate has melted, turn off the heat and leave it over the hot water to cool slowly.
3. Meanwhile, in a large mixing bowl, beat the butter or margarine with ¼ cup of the sugar until the mixture is fluffy and almost white. Add the egg yolks and beat for 1 minute. Add the almonds and brandy and beat for 2 minutes more.
4. In a separate bowl, beat the egg whites until light and foamy while grad-ually adding the remaining ¼ cup sugar. Continue beating the whites until they are stiff and shiny.

* You can use parve margarine, but Ann would not.

5. Add the cooled melted chocolate to the egg-yolk mixture and mix with a rubber spatula until well combined. Fold one quarter of this chocolate mixture into the egg whites; then gently fold this egg-white mixture back into the rest of the chocolate mixture, taking care not to deflate the batter.
6. Pour the batter into the prepared pan. Bake on the bottom rack of the oven for 25–30 minutes, or until a tester comes out covered with a thick, moist (not wet), and crumby coating.
7. Allow the cake to cool for 30 minutes in the pan. Loosen the edges with a knife, remove the sides, and carefully turn the cake upside down onto a plate. Remove the baking parchment. Sprinkle with the sugar.
8. Serve warm, at room temperature, or chilled with whipped cream and raspberries on the side.

Yield: 10–12 servings (D or P)

MERINGUE BASKETS
WITH LIME CREAM JEAN-LOUIS

FROM ANN AMERNICK

When I was growing up, my mother served a *schaum* (German for "foam") *torte* at our seder, straight from the *Settlement Cook Book*. This was a large meringue layered with strawberries. Ann Amernick's piquant lime cream scooped into individual meringue baskets makes a very unusual Passover offering. The lime cream recipe was adapted from that of Jean-Louis Palladin, the great chef at Restaurant Jean-Louis at the Watergate, Washington, D.C. Ann worked there as pastry chef for several years; unfortunately, the restaurant is now closed.

The lime cream:
>   Grated peel of 5 large limes
>   1 cup fresh lime juice
>   ½ cup (1 stick) unsalted butter or parve margarine
>   3 large eggs
>   3 large egg yolks
>   ¾ cup sugar

The meringue baskets:
>   8 large egg whites
>   1½ cups sugar

The lime cream:
1. Place the grated lime peel, the lime juice, and the butter or margarine in a 4-quart heavy-bottomed stainless-steel or enamel saucepan. Bring to a boil over medium heat; then remove from the heat.
2. In a medium bowl, mix the eggs, egg yolks, and sugar together until just combined. Do not beat.
3. Add 1 cup of the hot lime-and-butter mixture to the eggs, to warm them.

Stir and then add the egg mixture to the remaining lime-and-butter mixture in the pan.

4. Stir the mixture with a whisk over medium-high heat until thick and smooth, 5–8 minutes. Be sure to beat vigorously and touch all points of the bottom of the pan so you don't burn the mixture.

5. Strain the lime cream into a stainless-steel or glass bowl and quickly place a piece of plastic wrap over the cream to prevent a skin from forming. Cool to room temperature, then refrigerate until ready to use—it will keep for up to 2 weeks.

The meringue baskets:

6. In the bowl of an electric mixer, beat the egg whites with the whisk until light and foamy. Slowly add the sugar, 1 tablespoon at a time, until it has all been incorporated. Beat the meringue at medium speed for 8–10 minutes, until stiff and very glossy.

7. Preheat the oven to 200 degrees and cover 2 cookie sheets with greased baking parchment.

8. With an ice cream scoop or 2 large spoons, drop 18 mounds of the meringue on the cookie sheets, keeping each ball smooth. Make a deep pocket in each meringue by pushing the back of a spoon into the center

and using a blunt knife or the back of the spoon to push the meringue away from the center.

9. Bake the meringues on the middle rack of the oven for 1 hour. Turn off the oven and leave the meringues inside for 30 minutes more, or until dry. Cool them and, when ready to serve, fill each with 2 heaping tablespoons of the lime cream.

Yield: 3 cups lime cream (D or P), 18 meringue baskets (P)

PASSOVER SPONGE CAKE

FROM HELEN SILVERBERG

In a family known for good bakers, pastry chef Ann Amernick bows to her mother, Helen Silverberg, at Passover. "My mother is known for her sponge cakes because they are very light, high, and moist," she said. A classic sponge cake includes neither butter nor leavening agents. This one originated in Spain and became known throughout the Mediterranean as *pan de España de Pesah.* Make a great Passover trifle from any leftovers, soaked in liqueur and layered with fresh berries and cream.

9 large eggs, separated
1½ cups sugar
Grated peel and juice of 2 lemons
¾ cup matzah cake meal

1. Preheat the oven to 325 degrees and grease a 10-inch angel food or other tube pan.
2. In an electric mixer fitted with the whisk, beat the egg yolks at medium speed until light and fluffy, gradually adding the sugar. Continue beating and add the lemon peel and lemon juice. Add the matzah cake meal.
3. In a separate bowl, beat the egg whites at high speed until stiff. Then gently fold them into the egg-yolk mixture.
4. Pour the batter into the prepared pan and bake on the middle rack of the oven for 45 minutes, or until the sides of the cake pull away from the pan and the top springs back when lightly touched.
5. Remove the cake from the oven and let it cool completely before removing it from the pan. Serve this cake as is, or cut it into 2 layers and fill and decorate with strawberries. For a dairy meal, dot with a dollop of whipped cream.

Yield: 10–12 servings (P)

SHAVUOT

SPLENDID STRUDEL,
from Elisabeth Rosenfeld

SYRIAN CHEESE SAMBUSAK,
from Mansoura Middle Eastern Pastries

HUNGARIAN POGACSA,
from Alex Lichtman

MEA SHEARIM CHEESE DANISH,
from Brizel's Bakery

LEMON CHEESECAKE,
from Ann Amernick

POLISH-PARISIAN CHEESECAKE,
from Finkelsztajn's

So I have come down . . . to a land, goodly and spacious,
to a land flowing with milk and honey . . .

EXODUS 3:8

Shavuot, "the dairy holiday," comes in the late spring, the season of the most abundant milk and cheese products, the time when goats, sheep, and cows are grazing in new grass and thus producing more milk. Coming seven weeks after Passover, Shavuot originally celebrated the end of the barley harvest with a sacrificial offering of the first fruits at the Temple. Later, it came to commemorate the giving of the Ten Commandments at Mount Sinai.

The sacred mountain has six Hebrew names. One, Har Gavnunim, means "mountain of peaks." Since *gavnunim* comes from the same root as *givinah,* or "cheese," the name also means "cheese mountain," a popular folk image. Therefore, eating dairy dishes at this season is a reminder of the giving of the Law.

At the celebration of the barley harvest in ancient Israel, two loaves of bread were offered in the Temple. Since the Torah is also likened to bread, the long Shavuot loaf came to symbolize the length and breadth of the Law. These loaves often had four corners, symbolizing the four methods of interpreting the scriptural text: the simple, the esoteric, the homiletic, and the allegorical.

Strudel, Art from the Austro-Hungarian Empire

In 1939–40, when people could still leave Yugoslavia, a well-known chef taught many hopeful emigrants how to prepare intricate pastries so that they might be able to support themselves abroad. And when Diana Kennedy, the writer of Mexican cookbooks, wanted to learn to stretch strudel, she, like a whole generation of women (and some men) in Mexico City, took a class with Elisabeth Rosenfeld, one of those emigrants from Yugoslavia (see pages 120–21). Elisabeth's sister Aranka had been her teacher in the art of making strudel.

First the dough is mixed, thrown against a work surface, and set to rest until it is as flexible as taffy. Then the dough is placed in the middle of a large, cloth-covered table sprinkled with flour, patted out flat, and stretched with the fingers and the back of the hand until it is so thin you can read a newspaper through it. Holes do appear, but they are quickly patched up. The dough is finally sprinkled first with melted butter, then with fruit (or cheese, or a savory) and the excess dough is trimmed from the edges. The dough is then rolled up to form a three-inch-wide roll—the strudel—and baked.

Strudel is one of the Austro-Hungarian empire's great gifts to the world. Mrs. Rosenfeld, like other refugee women, earned a living from her skill.

For years I have been stretching strudel in my own home with my children. Before our elder daughter went off to college, she made a strudel each year for her school's auction and also gave strudels as gifts to her teachers. Now her younger sister has taken over. Making strudel is a cooperative enterprise, the culinary equivalent of a quilting bee. You need more than one person to stretch, preferably four. As the dough is carefully rolled out and then gradually pulled with the back of your hand and your fingers, it is a time to talk. The high-gluten flour and the warm butter or oil help to activate the dough, enabling it to stretch. Some people add vinegar as well, but Mrs. Rosenfeld did not. In Yugoslavia, she grew up using a goose feather to spread the melted butter on top of the roll as she turned the strudel; today we use a pastry brush.

This is a recipe for the adventurous. If you prefer the shortcut way, use the recipe on page 179, with bought phyllo dough.

SPLENDID STRUDEL

FROM ELISABETH ROSENFELD

2½ cups high-gluten flour*
1 large egg yolk
10 tablespoons (1 stick plus 2 tablespoons) unsalted butter or parve
    margarine, melted, or warm vegetable oil
Pinch of salt
¾ cup warm water
4 tablespoons dry breadcrumbs
Filling of choice (see below)
Confectioners' sugar for sprinkling

The dough:
1. Place a glass or ceramic bowl in a 150-degree oven while preparing the strudel dough.
2. If you are making the dough by hand, place in a large bowl the flour, egg yolk, 5 tablespoons of the melted butter, margarine, or oil, the salt, and the water. Mix thoroughly, adding more flour if the dough is too sticky. Then remove the dough from the bowl and work it by hitting it on a table sprinkled with flour until it no longer sticks to your fingers and you have a dough that is soft and elastic.
   If you are using a food processor, fit it with the steel blade and put in the flour, egg yolk, 5 tablespoons of the melted butter, margarine, or oil, the salt, and the water and pulse, adding more flour if needed, until you have a smooth, soft dough.
3. Remove the warmed bowl from the oven and grease with some of the melted butter, margarine, or oil. Grease the dough, too; then place it on a board sprinkled with flour and cover with the bowl. Allow the covered dough to rest in a warm place for 30 minutes. (This is a technique I have

* Available from King Arthur Flour, *The Baker's Catalogue* (see page 202).

found over and over in old cookbooks.) Now prepare the filling (see pages 179–82), so it is ready after you've stretched the dough.

Stretching the dough:
4. Cover a 5-foot-long table with a clean sheet and sprinkle the sheet with flour. Using a rolling pin, roll out the dough gradually until it measures about 10 by 20 inches. Then, using 2, 3, or 4 people spaced evenly around a table, gently lift the dough with the palms of your hands. Carefully extend the dough with the tips of your fingers, then with the back of your hands, until it is as thin as possible in all places, measuring about 30 by 30 inches. (This is not a recipe for long fingernails.) Trim off the thick edges of the stretched dough with a knife; let the dough sit for about 4 minutes. This waiting period is important, since it helps make a crisper strudel. Don't worry about tears—just patch them up with the leftover dough. Give the rest to children to sprinkle with sugar and cinnamon and then bake.

Filling and baking the strudel:
5. Leaving a 2-inch border all around and a 4-inch-wide strip up the middle, drizzle some melted butter, margarine, or oil over the dough; then sprinkle on the breadcrumbs, and finally spread the filling over the dough.
6. Preheat the oven to 375 degrees; line a 12- by 15-inch baking pan with aluminum foil (you need the foil for removing the strudel).
7. With the help of the sheet, and with the bare strip of dough perpendicular to you, carefully and tightly roll up the strudel like a jelly roll. Using a sharp knife or a pastry scraper, divide the long strudel into two 15-inch strudels at the point in the center where the strudel dough is unfilled, twist the open ends to close, and cut off the excess dough at the ends. Carefully, using both your hands or 2 sets of hands, remove the 2 strudels to the lined pan. Brush again with the butter, margarine, or oil.
8. Bake the strudels on the middle rack of the oven for 35 minutes, or until golden.
9. Sprinkle with confectioners' sugar and cut into slices 3 fingers thick, about 1½ inches. Serve warm; for a dairy meal, serve with with vanilla ice cream, whipped cream, or vanilla frozen yogurt.

Yield: two 15-inch-long strudels, 6–8 servings each (D or P)

NOTE: If you want to bake them later, you can freeze the unbaked strudels, wrapped. Remove from the freezer 30 minutes before baking. Then bake as above and serve warm. You can also form and bake the strudels early in the day, and then reheat them at 375 degrees for 10 minutes just before serving.

VARIATION: SHORTCUT STRUDEL

4 sheets prepared phyllo dough
½ cup (1 stick) unsalted butter or parve margarine, melted
Filling of choice (see below)
Confectioners' sugar

1. Preheat the oven to 375 degrees and grease a jelly-roll pan.
2. Take 1 sheet of phyllo and spread it out on a work surface. (Cover the rest of the dough while working the sheet.) Brush with the melted butter or margarine. Place a second phyllo sheet on top. Brush with butter or margarine.
3. Spread half the filling mixture over the entire surface of the phyllo, leaving a 1-inch border. Starting with the long side, carefully roll the phyllo, jelly-roll fashion, ending with the seam on the bottom. Brush the top with more butter or margarine and place in the jelly-roll pan. Repeat steps 2 and 3 with the 2 remaining phyllo sheets.
4. Bake the strudels on the middle rack of the oven for 35 minutes, or until golden. Just before serving, sprinkle with confectioners' sugar. Serve warm. For a dairy meal, serve with ice cream, frozen yogurt, or whipped cream.

Yield: 2 strudels, 12–14 servings (D or P)

NOTE: You can freeze these strudels also, wrapped, after assembling them. Remove from the freezer 30 minutes before baking them.

Apple Filling

10–12 Granny Smith, Jonathan, or other good baking apples, peeled,
 cored, and grated (about 10 cups)
Juice of 1 lemon
⅓ cup raisins (optional)
Grated peel of 1 lemon
2 teaspoons cinnamon
1 cup sugar
½ cup coarsely ground walnuts or almonds (ground in a food
 processor)

1. Sprinkle the grated apples with lemon juice and place in a colander over
    a plate until ready to use. Press the apples to release any excess moisture.
    This is important to a successful strudel.
2. Mix the apples with the raisins and lemon peel in a bowl.
3. Following the instructions in step 5, page 178, spread the apple mixture
    over the breadcrumb layer on the stretched strudel dough and dust with
    the cinnamon. Sprinkle the sugar and then the ground nuts over the
    apples and cinnamon. Roll and bake as above.

Yield: filling for 2 strudels (P)

Cherry Filling

10 cups sour cherries, pitted, or five 16-ounce cans sour cherries, well
 drained
2 cups sugar
½ cup ground almonds or walnuts

1. Place the pitted cherries in a colander over a plate until ready to use.
2. Following the instructions in step 5, page 178, scatter the cherries over
    the breadcrumb layer on the stretched-out strudel dough. Sprinkle with
    the sugar and finally the ground nuts. Roll and bake as above.

Yield: filling for 2 strudels (P)

NOTE: You can use other fruits, such as rhubarb. Just make sure you drain them very well to remove as much liquid as possible.

Sweet Cheese Filling

    2 large egg yolks
    2 large eggs, separated
    1½ cups sugar
    1 pound plus 5 ounces farmer cheese
    1 cup sour cream
    Grated peel of 1 lemon
    ½ cup raisins

1. In a food processor fitted with the steel blade, purée 3 of the egg yolks with half of the sugar, the farmer cheese, and ½ cup of the sour cream.
2. Add the lemon peel and raisins; pulse briefly to mix them in. Remove the mixture to a large bowl.
3. Beat the egg whites until stiff, gradually adding the remaining sugar, and then gently fold them into the yolk mixture.
4. Following the instructions in step 5, page 178, spread the filling over the breadcrumb layer on the stretched strudel dough. Roll as above.
5. In a small bowl, combine the remaining ½ cup sour cream with the remaining egg yolk and mix well. Spread this over the top of the rolled-up strudel and bake as above.

Yield: filling for 2 strudels (D)

Cabbage Filling

I love strudel made with this Hungarian sautéed cabbage filling and serve it frequently as a first course for dinner parties. People are always surprised at the combination of cabbage, caraway, and onions inside a strudel.

    1 head of white cabbage (2 pounds)
    2 teaspoons salt
    4 tablespoons vegetable oil

1 medium onion, coarsely chopped
Freshly ground black pepper to taste
1 teaspoon caraway seeds (optional)
1 tablespoon sugar
1 teaspoon cinnamon

1. Remove the core from the cabbage and shred it, using a food processor or grater.
2. Sprinkle the shredded cabbage with the salt and let stand about 15 minutes. Squeeze out the excess water.
3. Place the 4 tablespoons oil in a heavy frying pan. Brown the onions until golden. Remove the onions from the pan and set aside. Sauté the cabbage, cooking carefully until wilted (you will probably have to do this in 2 batches). Combine the cabbage and onions in a bowl and drain off any liquid.
4. Following the instructions in step 5, page 178, spread the cabbage-onion mixture over the breadcrumb layer on the stretched strudel dough. Sprinkle with the pepper, caraway seeds, sugar, and cinnamon, adjusting the seasoning to taste. Roll and bake as above.

Yield: filling for 2 strudels (P)

SYRIAN CHEESE SAMBUSAK (Cheese Turnovers)

FROM MANSOURA MIDDLE EASTERN PASTRIES

A Syrian Jewish home today would not be Syrian without a freezer filled with cheese *sambusak.* "Syrian women make them for breakfast, for a card game, for a brit or a bar mitzvah," said Josiane Mansoura, whose store (see pages 96–97) is always stocked with these filled crescent-shaped pastries. "More are eaten at Shavuot than at any other holiday."

Originally stuffed with the goat cheese of Syria, *sambusak* can be made with Muenster, the Balkan cheese *kashkeval,* or any hard gratable cheese. Semolina adds a crunchy texture to the dough, which in this particular version is baked, a healthier alternative to the traditional fried version. *Sambusak* stuffed with chicken or potatoes are eaten as well by Indian, Iraqi, and Persian Jews.

The dough:
- 1½ cups *smead** (semolina, not semolina flour)
- 3 cups unbleached all-purpose flour
- Dash of salt
- 3 tablespoons vegetable oil
- ¾ cup (1½ sticks) unsalted butter, at room temperature
- ¾ cup cold water

The filling:[†]
- 4 large eggs
- 2 pounds Muenster, grated, or, for a tangier filling, 3 parts grated Muenster to 1 part crumbled feta cheese
- Dash of salt
- 2 cups sesame seeds

---

[*] Available at Middle Eastern markets.
[†] See also the spinach filling on page 185.

The dough:

1. Mix the semolina with the all-purpose flour in a large bowl. Add the salt, oil, and butter. With a fork or your fingers, work in the butter until the dough is lumpy; do not overmix. Add the water, a little at a time, bringing the dough together until it is smooth and pliable. (You can also make the dough in a food processor fitted with the steel blade, pulsing as you mix the butter in and then the water a little at a time.) Set the dough aside.

Filling and assembling the sambusak:

2. Beat the eggs and combine with the grated cheese and salt. The mixture should be slightly dry.
3. Preheat the oven to 350 degrees and oil 2 cookie sheets.
4. Place the sesame seeds on a large plate. Tear the dough into walnut-sized pieces and roll them with your hands into 1-inch balls. Flatten them slightly and dip one side into the sesame seeds. Then flatten to an ⅛-inch thickness with a rolling pin, your hands, or a tortilla press. If using

a tortilla press, cover with plastic wrap so the dough doesn't stick to the press.

5. With the sesame-seed side of the dough circle facing down, place 1 table-spoon of the filling in the middle of the circle. Fold one side over the other to form a half moon. Press the edges to close, and crimp them, if desired. Place the *sambusak* on the 2 cookie sheets, leaving ½ inch between them.

6. Bake the *sambusak* for 20–25 minutes on the middle and lower racks of the oven until slightly golden, switching racks after 10 minutes. Do not overcook.

Yield: about 60 sambusak (D)

VARIATION: SPINACH FILLING

20 ounces fresh spinach, cleaned and chopped
4 ounces goat cheese, crumbled
Salt and freshly ground pepper

Fill each *sambusak* with 1 tablespoon spinach and ½ teaspoon goat cheese. Lightly sprinkle with salt and pepper. Fold over, seal, and bake as above.

HUNGARIAN POGACSA (Sweet Biscuits)

FROM ALEX LICHTMAN

I will never forget the first time I tasted *pogacsa* at the home of Cissie Klavens, the daughter of Alex Lichtman (see pages 88–89). She served them with homemade apricot jam. Since then, these round buttery biscuits, a cross between a scone and a brioche, have become my special-occasion breakfast treat. They are also wonderful with tea.

George Lang, the doyen of Hungarian cuisine, serves tiny versions of *pogacsa* as hors d'oeuvres at his Gundel's Restaurant in Budapest. Alex Lichtman used to make his with *griebenes* (rendered goose-fat cracklings) in the old Hungarian Jewish way. Originally a simple wheat bread baked in ashes, coming from the Turkish *bogaca*, *pogacsa* became progressively enriched through the centuries until its present glorious state, translated below.

1 scant tablespoon (1 package) active dry yeast
3 tablespoons warm milk
1 cup (2 sticks) unsalted butter, at room temperature
3½ cups unbleached all-purpose flour
1 teaspoon salt
¼ teaspoon vanilla extract
¼ cup plus 2 tablespoons sugar
½ cup sour cream
2 large egg yolks
1 large egg, beaten

1. In a small bowl, mix the yeast with the warm milk.
2. In an electric mixer fitted with the paddle, beat together the butter, 3 cups of the flour, the salt, and the vanilla on low speed for 2 minutes.
3. Add the sugar and continue beating on low speed for 2 more minutes. Add the sour cream, yeast mixture, and egg yolks. Continue beating on low speed for 3 minutes more, then 2 more minutes on medium speed. The dough will form a ball quickly.

4. Place the dough on a work surface covered with the remaining ½ cup flour and roll it out to a rectangle about 9 by 13 inches, ½ inch thick. Working from the shorter side, fold one third of the dough up; then fold the top third of the dough down and over it, like a business letter. Refrigerate in a lightly floured pan for 15 minutes. Then repeat the procedure: Roll out the dough again, fold again, and refrigerate again for 15 minutes.

5. Roll out the dough to a rectangle ⅓ inch thick and brush with the beaten egg. This time, fold the 2 shorter ends of the rectangle in to meet at the center, then fold in half the other way. Cover and refrigerate the dough overnight.

6. Remove the dough from the refrigerator and let it soften about 10 minutes before rolling. Then roll the dough out on a lightly floured board to a rectangle about 8 by 10 inches, ¾ inch thick. For decoration, use the tip of a knife to gently draw diagonal lines about ¼ inch apart to make a grid or crisscross pattern.

7. Using a floured 2-inch round cookie cutter, cut out circles of dough and place them on 2 greased cookie sheets. Scrape up dough scraps, roll out again, and cut more biscuits. Brush the biscuits with the beaten egg; then allow them to rise and dry for 35 minutes.

8. Preheat the oven to 350 degrees. Again, lightly brush the biscuits with the beaten egg.

9. Bake the *pogacsa* on the middle rack of the oven for 20–25 minutes, or until lightly golden. Serve with apricot jam.

Yield: about 20 pogacsa *(D)*

MEA SHEARIM CHEESE DANISH

FROM BRIZEL'S BAKERY

This old-fashioned cheese Danish, made with a buttery yeast dough and filled with farmer cheese, is one of the most popular pastries at this well-known Jerusalem bakery (see page 19 for more about Brizel's Bakery). Mr. Brizel let me watch the process of smearing butter onto the dough and then folding it in. He shared the recipe with me before he ran off to late-morning prayers with his father.

Retired baker Fred Loeb kindly spent a day teaching me how to translate this process into a great cheese Danish.

Unfortunately, Danish making is a dying art. In most bakeries today, the convenient commercial puff pastry and cream cheese have replaced Danish dough and the authentic farmer cheese filling.

The dough:
    ¾ cup sugar
    ½ cup (1 stick) plus 2 tablespoons unsalted butter, parve margarine,
        or vegetable shortening, at room temperature
    ½ teaspoon salt
    ½ teaspoon vanilla extract
    Grated peel of ½ lemon
    3 large eggs
    1 large egg yolk
    1½ cups cold water
    1 scant tablespoon (1 package) active dry yeast
    4 cups unbleached all-purpose flour, plus more for sprinkling
    ¼ cup slivered toasted almonds for garnish (optional)
    Confectioners' sugar for garnish (optional)

The filling:
　1½ pounds farmer cheese, drained
　3 cups sugar
　6 tablespoons unsalted butter
　3 large eggs
　Pinch of salt
　⅓ cup unbleached all-purpose flour
　1½ teaspoons vanilla extract

The dough:

1. In the bowl of an electric mixer fitted with the paddle, cream ¼ cup of the sugar with ¼ cup of the butter, margarine, or vegetable shortening, the salt, vanilla, and lemon peel. Add 2 of the eggs, the egg yolk, and 1 cup of the water and mix well, about 4 minutes.

2. Attach the dough hook and gradually add the yeast and flour as you continue mixing for about 5 minutes at medium speed. The dough will be very sticky.

3. Sprinkle flour on your hands and on the dough, remove the dough from the bowl, and place it on a floured surface. Gently pat the dough out into a rectangle about 6 by 8 inches and fold it in half over itself. Repeat this process about 6 times, turning the dough a quarter turn each time. Then, still using your hands, pat the dough into a rectangle about 8 by 10 inches. Cut up the remaining butter into tiny pieces and place on two thirds of the dough, leaving a shorter side free of butter. Take this unbuttered third and fold over the center third. Then take the remaining one third and fold it over the center third. You will now have dough folded in thirds, like a business letter.

4. Roll the dough out with a rolling pin to a rectangle about 8 by 14 inches. Fold in thirds from a shorter side, dusting off the excess flour. Let the dough rest for 5 minutes.

5. Roll the dough out again to another rectangle 8 by 14 inches and fold in thirds from a shorter side, as above. Cover the dough with a towel and let it rest for 15 minutes in the refrigerator. Repeat this rolling and folding in thirds process 3 more times and refrigerate. A baker's trick to help remember which roll you are on is to use your thumb to make 1, 2, 3, or 4 indentations in the dough.

6. Refrigerate at least 30 minutes or overnight.

Filling and baking the Danish:

7. Put all the ingredients for the filling in a food processor fitted with the steel blade. Pulse just until smooth. Refrigerate for several hours.

8. Take one half of the dough and roll it out on a lightly floured board to a rectangle 11 by 14 inches, ¼ inch thick. Whisk the remaining egg in a small bowl to make an egg wash. Brush this wash over the dough surface. Spread with half the cheese filling, leaving a 1-inch border. From a longer side, fold one third over the middle third, and then fold the remaining third over the dough. Brush the top with the egg wash. Repeat this process with the other half of the dough. Let the Danish rise, covered, for

| Brush dough surface with egg wash | Spread with filling, leaving 1-inch border | Fold | Brush egg wash over top of Danish |

another hour on a greased cookie sheet. (In place of this rising, you can freeze the Danish at this point. Defrost 4 hours at room temperature, on a greased cookie sheet, before baking.)

9. Preheat the oven to 400 degrees. Place the 2 Danish on the middle rack and bake for 20 minutes, or until golden brown.

Topping the Danish:

10. While the Danish are baking, place the remaining ½ cup water and ½ cup sugar in a saucepan to make a syrup. Bring it to a boil and let it boil for 3–4 minutes uncovered. Turn off the heat.

11. Remove the Danish from the oven and brush the warm syrup over them. Scatter slivered almonds on top or dust with confectioners' sugar. Let the Danish cool before serving them. Better yet, serve them the next day.

Yield: 2 large Danish (D)

VARIATION: INDIVIDUAL DANISH

1. Once you have completed steps 1–6 above, roll out one half of the dough on a lightly floured board to a square about 16 by 16 inches, ⅛ inch thick. Cut into 4-inch squares, brush each with the egg wash, and place a heaping tablespoon of filling in the center of each square. Fold 2 opposite corners in over the filling so they meet at the center, and then the other 2 opposite corners. Brush again with the egg wash. Repeat this process with the other half of the dough. Remove to 2 greased cookie sheets. Let the Danish sit about 1 hour, covered.

2. Preheat the oven to 400 degrees.

3. Place the Danish on the cookie sheets and bake them 15–20 minutes, or until golden brown. Follow instructions under "Topping the Danish" above.

Yield: 32 individual Danish (D)

LEMON CHEESECAKE

FROM ANN AMERNICK

For many Americans, New York cheesecake means the rich Jewish cream cheese cake that originated at Lindy's and Reuben's restaurants. To make a great one, there is no substitute for good-quality ingredients—real vanilla extract, the best cream cheese and sour cream. This version has a very smooth and pleasingly tart filling. I love Ann's addition of walnuts to the crust.

The crust:
    ½ cup walnuts
    ⅓ cup sugar
    ½ cup (1 stick) unsalted butter, cold
    1 cup unbleached all-purpose flour

The filling:
    2 pounds cream cheese, at room temperature
    ¾ cup sugar
    4 large eggs
    2 large egg yolks
    1 cup sour cream
    Grated peel and juice of 1 lemon
    1 teaspoon vanilla extract
    3 tablespoons unbleached all-purpose flour

The topping:
    2 cups sour cream, at room temperature
    2 teaspoons vanilla extract
    2 tablespoons sugar

The crust:

1. Grind the nuts with 1 tablespoon of the sugar in a food processor fitted with the steel blade. Cut up the butter and add the pieces, with the remaining sugar and the flour, to the processor. Process, pulsing, until a ball of dough is formed.
2. Wrap the dough in plastic wrap and refrigerate for 30 minutes.
3. Preheat the oven to 350 degrees and press the dough onto the bottom of a greased 10-inch springform pan.
4. Bake the crust on the middle rack of the oven for 20–25 minutes, or until golden in color. Remove from the oven and let cool. Leave the oven on.

Filling and baking the cheesecake:

5. Put the cream cheese in the bowl of an electric mixer and beat with the whisk on the lowest speed for about 10 minutes, or until soft and smooth, while gradually adding the sugar and scraping the sides occasionally. This long, slow action will give the filling a silky texture.
6. Add the eggs, egg yolks, sour cream, lemon peel and juice, and vanilla; mix again on the lowest speed for a few minutes, scraping the sides and beaters frequently. Then gradually add the flour.
7. Scoop the cream-cheese mixture onto the prepared crust. Place a pan of water in the oven on the lowest rack. Turn the oven down to 325 degrees and bake the cheesecake on the middle rack for 1¼–1½ hours.
8. Remove the cheesecake from the oven and let it cool for 10–15 minutes. Do not turn off the oven.

Topping the cheesecake:

9. Put the sour cream, vanilla, and sugar in a bowl and mix well. Spoon the mixture evenly over the top of the slightly cooled cheesecake.
10. Return the cheesecake to the oven for 10 minutes. After removing it, let it cool, remove the sides of the springform, and transfer it to a serving plate.

Yield: one 10-inch cheesecake (D)

POLISH-PARISIAN CHEESECAKE

FROM FINKELSZTAJN'S

This is the way Jewish cheesecake must have tasted in Lodz, Poland. Before Jews came to America they used a rich farmer cheese instead of our processed cream cheese. After tasting this cheesecake from Finkelsztajn's Bakery in Paris (see pages 70–71), I went to a market near the bakery, bought a wheel of farmer cheese, and carried it back to the United States— just so I could test the real recipe. Although our commercial farmer cheese does well as a substitute, nothing really takes the place of cheese fresh from the farm.

The crust:
 ⅓ cup unsalted butter, cold
 ¼ cup sugar
 Dash of salt
 1⅓ cups unbleached all-purpose flour
 4 tablespoons ice water

The filling:
 ½ cup raisins (optional)
 ½ cup milk
 Three 7½-ounce packages farmer cheese, at room temperature
 ½ cup unbleached all-purpose flour
 5 large eggs, separated
 ⅔ cup sugar
 Grated peel of 1 lemon
 2 tablespoons lemon juice
 1 teaspoon vanilla extract
 Dash of salt
 ½ cup slivered almonds

The crust:
1. Use a food processor fitted with the steel blade to combine the butter and sugar, pulsing. Add the salt and flour, pulse, then add the ice water and pulse until a ball is formed, adding more flour if it is too sticky. Remove the dough, wrap in plastic wrap, and refrigerate for about an hour.

Filling and baking the cheesecake:
2. Drop the raisins into the milk and let them sit for 1 hour.
3. Drain the raisins, reserving the milk. Combine the milk with the cheese, flour, egg yolks, sugar, lemon peel and juice, vanilla, and salt in a food processor; pulse to blend thoroughly. Remove to a bowl and stir in the raisins.
4. Beat the egg whites until stiff peaks form and fold them into the cheese mixture.
5. Preheat the oven to 350 degrees and butter a 9-inch springform pan. Quickly press the crust dough into the bottom and 2 inches up the sides. Pour the filling into the crust and sprinkle with the almonds.
6. Bake the cheesecake on the middle rack of the oven for 40 minutes, or until a toothpick comes out clean when inserted in the center. Cool in the pan for 15 minutes before removing the springform sides. Chill and serve garnished with fresh mint and fruit.

Yield: one 9-inch cheesecake (D)

GLOSSARY OF FOREIGN FOOD TERMS

adjwah Short for *erass b'adjwah*, a Syrian semolina-and-flour-dough pocket stuffed with dates

afikomen A piece of matzah broken off from the middle of three matzot used at the Passover seder and set aside until the end of the meal

apfelkuchen German apple cake

babka An Eastern European cake made from an egg-and-butter yeast-based dough, often filled with chocolate or cinnamon-sugar and nuts

berches A German and Central European challah often made from potatoes

biscocho A Sephardic biscuit with a hole, often filled with coriander or anise seeds and then dipped in sesame seeds

biscotti Italian *mandelbrot*

bogaca A Turkish form of *pogacsa*

bollo A Spanish word for a bun, bread, or small cake

boyos Puff pastries of Turkish origin, often shaped like a snail and filled with potatoes, spinach, and/or cheese

brioche A yeast-based butter-and-egg-rich bread of French origin

burekas Triangular or sometimes round pastries of Turkish origin, filled with spinach, cheese, eggplant, or meat

cholent A slow-baked Sabbath stew of meat, potatoes, and beans

croquembouche French pastry, often cream puffs, mounded together with a sugar glaze

crozette The French word for *biscocho*

dobos torte A classic Hungarian seven-layer cake filled with chocolate buttercream and usually topped with a caramel glaze

fijuelas Moroccan deep-fried pastries dipped in honey

fluden A German and Central European double- and sometimes multi-layered pastry filled with apples, nuts, and other fruits

gesundheitskuchen A southern German cake; the word means "good health cake"

hamantashen Triangular Purim cookies filled with prunes, poppy seeds, nuts, or even chocolate chips

haroset A paste-like mixture of fruits, nuts, cinnamon, and wine eaten during the Passover seder and symbolic of the mortar the Israelites used in building during the Egyptian slavery

ka'ak A Syrian savory biscuit, also called *biscocho*

kichel The Yiddish word for "cookie," either savory or sweet

kindli Hungarian cookies for Purim

kneidlach Soup dumplings made from matzah meal, eggs, chicken fat, and sometimes ground almonds, usually boiled but sometimes fried

krimsel Deep-fried fritters made from matzah or matzah meal and served at Passover

kubbanah A Yemenite overnight bread, typically served on the Sabbath

kugel A baked sweet or savory pudding or casserole made of noodles, potatoes, bread, or vegetables and often served on the Sabbath or festivals, traditionally baked in a round container

kugelhopf A Central European cake made from an egg-and-sugar yeast dough, often filled with cinnamon-sugar and nuts

lavash A cracker-like Middle Eastern flat bread

lechem The Hebrew word for "bread"

loukomades   Greek deep-fried pastries dipped in honey

macarones   The Spanish word for "macaroons"

mahlep   A Middle Eastern term for the ground centers of cherry pits

mahmoul   Middle Eastern cookies filled with nuts and sometimes dates

malai   The Yiddish word for "cornmeal," borrowed from Romanian

mandelbrot   Almond bread of Eastern or Central European origin

matzah   Unleavened "bread of affliction and freedom" eaten at Passover

mishloach manot   Food portions consisting of at least one fruit and one sweet made from flour, given at Purim

mürbeteig   A German butter-cookie dough often used as a base for fruit-filled pies

oznei Haman   "Haman's ears," Middle Eastern deep-fried pastry served with sugar at Purim

pan de España de Pesah   Passover lemon sponge cake of Sephardic origin

pane de Sabato   The Ladino term for "Sabbath bread"

pfannkuchen   A German or Austrian doughnut, often filled with jam

pletzel   Short for Bialystoker *tzibele pletzel,* a flat onion bread originally from the city of Bialystok, Poland

pogacsa   Hungarian term for a biscuit or bread

sambusak   A crescent-shaped pastry, filled with savories, from Syria and Iraq

schaum torte   A German meringue torte often filled with strawberries and/or whipped cream

schnecken   A snail-shaped yeast dough filled with nuts, sugar, cinnamon, and sometimes raisins and baked

smead   Semolina

strudel   Central European stretched dough filled with fruit, cheese, nuts, or savories

sufganiyot   Jelly doughnuts served in Israel at Chanukah

taiglach   Pieces of fried dough coated in honey, traditionally served at Rosh Hashanah

travados   The Sephardic version of *sambusak,* nut-filled, crescent-shaped cookies

zelebi   A Tunisian honey-coated pastry

zwetschgenkuchen   An Alsatian and southern German tart made with a short crust and filled with Italian plums

SHOPPING GUIDE

Ann Amernick
Chevy Chase, Maryland
Phone: 301-718-0434
Special-occasion and Passover dairy cakes (special orders only)

Brizel's Bakery
68 Mea Shearim Street, Jerusalem, Israel
Open 7:00 a.m. to 8:00 p.m. Sunday through Thursday, and 7:00 a.m.
until 2 hours before sunset on Friday
Challah, Danish, cookies, cakes

Elat Grocery
8730 West Pico Boulevard, Los Angeles, California 90035
Phone: 310-659-7070
Open 8:00 a.m. to 8:00 p.m., Sunday through Thursday
Middle Eastern kosher spices and baking items

Fairmount Bagel Bakery Inc.
74 West Fairmount Street, Montreal, Quebec H2T 2M2
Phone: 514-272-0667
Open 24 hours a day
Bagels, bozo bagels

Finkelsztajn's Bakery
27 rue des Rosiers, Paris
Phone: 47-727-891
24 rue des Ecouffes, Paris
Phone: 48-879-285
Cheesecakes, *fluden, pletzel*

Heavenly Hallah

P.O. Box 47, Lincolnshire, Illinois 60069
Phone: 847-680-2200
Challah, honey cake, gift baskets (special orders only)

King Arthur Flour

The Baker's Catalogue
P.O. Box 876, Norwich, Vermont 05055
Phone: 800-827-6836
High-gluten, rye, and other bread flours

Edda Servi Machlin's books

Giro Press, P.O. Box 203, Croton-on-Hudson, New York 10520
Phone: 914-271-8924

Mansoura Middle Eastern Pastries

515 Kings Highway, Brooklyn, New York 11223
Phone: 718-645-7977
Open 9:00 a.m. to 6:30 p.m. Sunday through Thursday, 9:00 a.m. until 1 hour before Shabbat on Friday
Syrian Jewish kosher bakery specialties, including *ka'ak, adjwah,* baklava

Star Bakery

26031 Coolidge, Oak Park, Michigan 48237
Phone: 810-541-9450
Open 6:00 a.m. to 7:30 p.m. Monday through Saturday, 6:00 a.m. to 6:00 p.m. Sunday
Rye breads, challah, *kichel,* babka, kaiser rolls

Walnut Acres Organic Farms

Penns Creek, Pennsylvania 17862
Phone: 800-433-3998
Open 24 hours a day
Yeasts and flours

Williams-Sonoma

P.O. Box 7256, San Francisco, California 94120

Phone: 800-541-2233

Open 7:30 a.m. to 9:00 p.m. EST

Good-quality chocolate, baking ware

Zingerman's Bake House

422 Detroit Street, P.O. Box 1868

Ann Arbor, Michigan 48106-1868

Phone: 313-769-1625; fax: 313-769-1235

Order by e-mail: zing@chamber.ann-arbor.mi.us

Open 9:00 a.m. to 5:00 p.m. EST

INDEX

※

ABOUT THE AUTHOR

Joan Nathan's books include *The Jewish Holiday Kitchen*, *The Children's Jewish Holiday Kitchen*, and *Jewish Cooking in America*, which won the IACP Julia Child Award for Best Cookbook of the Year in 1995 and the James Beard Award for Best American Cookbook. She contributes articles on international ethnic food and special holiday features to the *New York Times*, the Los Angeles Times Syndicate, *Hadassah Magazine*, *Food and Wine*, and *Food Arts*. She lives in Washington, D.C., with her husband, Allan Gerson, and three children.